ENDORSEMENTS

"Engaging, timely, impactful. A must read."
Ken Pink
President and Chief Operating Officer, EW James
Union City, TN

"Are you looking for a book that will give you hope for a better life? This is it."
Erin Fletcher
Director, Human Resources
Cambric Corporation
Salt Lake City, Utah

"When facing challenges in my life, I often turn to Kip for guidance. His journey and personal transformation has provided him with wisdom and a perspective on life that few others have. By reading his book, many will benefit as I have."
Jack Sullivan
Chief Financial Officer, Mercantile Partners
Chicago, Il

"A true story that will change your life.
Ber
Harvard Law Student, cla
B

THE IMPOSTER

HOW A JUVENILE CRIMINAL SUCCEEDED IN BUSINESS AND LIFE

By

KIP KREILING

The Imposter

Library of Congress Catalog Card Number – Pending

Second Printing

ISBN 978-0-615-32055-7

TransformationHelp Press

Additional books can be ordered at
www.KipKreiling.com

Please send correspondence or requests for speaking engagements to:

Kip@KipKreiling.com

Cover art by: Heather Carter / RainstormArt
Cover design by Allen Dellinger

Printed in USA
by Publishers Printing

To my Mother

More than anyone,
she tried to hold my hand when I was determined to
walk on very dark and dangerous roads.

Today, she joins me in my celebration of life.

All of the events about the author described in this book are true. When relevant, the actual dates and locations have been provided.

Some of the names were changed to protect the identity of people and companies that did not provide permission for their real names to be used. For more details, please refer to the Chapter Notes at the back of the book.

Table of Contents

Chapter		Page
1	THE IMPOSTER	1
2	BURNING BOATS	57
3	TRAPPED BY A CURTAIN OF IDEAS	87
4	MIND TO MUSCLE TO METAMORPHOSIS	121
5	THE FIRE PRECEDES THE BLOOM	173
6	REALITY SLICING	207
7	TRAGEDY AT THE ALTAR	241
	ACKNOWLEDGEMENTS	285
	CHAPTER NOTES	290
	ABOUT THE AUTHOR	304

CHAPTER ONE

THE IMPOSTER

Her radiant smile catches me off guard. The waitresses in this place are instructed to be pleasant, but her face is different from the others. Her smile is not false. Her expression is honest. Her slender figure seems to glide across the carpeted dining room, weaving between the tables where the other executives are sitting in this private dining room.

She continues toward me and I realize, very unsettled, that she is smiling at *me*.

"Would you like the appetizer Rillette de Lapin, pruneaux au Cognac?" I detect a tremor in her demeanor, both in her smile and in her eyes. She is uncertain of something. Old fears begin to play like a silent horror film in my head. Does this waitress, this young girl, suspect that I do not belong here? Does this young woman, who knows nothing about me, suspect that I am an imposter? Of course not! How absurd! I must be losing my mind. Then again, it makes sense to me. She's the type of person that would understand a guy like me. It would be simple for her to detect me – like hearing an out-of-tune instrument disrupting an elegant orchestra.

I imagine the people that she has served in this place. As I look around, I see so many fortunate faces that have been carefully chiseled – personalities that have been nurtured and shaped by the finishing schools and influences of high society. From her perspective, it must be quite obvious: I do not belong in this world. I am something entirely different. Am I a wolf in sheep's clothing? Perhaps I am a spy in their midst. Somehow, I have found my way out of the gutter, but am I doomed to kneel and beg among the rich and privileged?

"Sir, your appetizer?"

Before I can respond, she quickly defines the menu item.

"The Rabbit Rillettes are cooked in prune brandy, sir."

Why did she give me the definition in English? Has she assumed that I do not understand French? I am sure that many patrons in this restaurant understand French menu items without needing the definition in English. Why did she explain it to me? Perhaps this young lady is more perceptive than my esteemed coworkers. Perhaps she has eyes like knives. Have her eyes penetrated my cool exterior of neatly groomed professionalism?

"Thank you, I will have the Rillettes," I said, clearing my throat and laughing to my friends at the table, implying that the definition was entirely unnecessary. "I hope I like the Rillettes. I have never tried them before, nor do I have the faintest idea what they are."

Sweat has formed on my brow, probably unnoticeable unless I was closely scrutinized through a magnifying glass. To hide my anxiety, I casually touch my forehead with a napkin.

It is mid December 2005 and just outside the nearby walls of this elegant dining room the ground is cold and frozen. Crystallized snow flakes connect in an unending sea of white that blankets the ground. I am in downtown Minneapolis, one of the locations on this planet that was not designed for human habitation, at least not in the winter.

In this city, weeks can pass between the months of November and February where the thermometer never rises above negative 10 degrees. To help protect the city's inhabitants from the frigid winter spells, many of the downtown buildings are connected by translucent tubes – tubes that appear to hover above the streets. Like a space-age city, a person can walk several miles in downtown Minneapolis in these tubes, from building to building, and never set foot on a sidewalk. After a few hours of traveling this way, the city begins to feel like a giant frozen hamster cage. For some, this would be a terrible nightmare; they would feel like human hamsters scurrying around in plastic tubes. For others, it is has become an accepted way of living.

Then again, most of my fellow dinner guests hardly ever use the tubes. They move around this city, and the other cities they frequent, in limousines or in the back seat of a Rolls Royce, piloted by private chauffeurs.

I'm suddenly struck by a daydream: What kind of world is this? Translucent tubes and sky-scrapers gnaw at the sky like fangs. Minneapolis is the typical modern city. It is occupied by American executives as well as addicts, common crooks, and the wretched poor. Along the same frozen streets the sharks in suits and the sharks in rags swim and hunt and kill. But it was not always this way. Or perhaps it was. It is hard for a man to decide.

I look at a nearby window and contemplate the frozen world outside. The building I am sitting in came from another age, a time I am not at all familiar with. The outside walls of this building are made of stone, which was carefully carved by human hands. Even a small child walking down the street would recognize that this building no longer matches the tubes and stainless steel structures of this city.

I am having dinner inside the Minneapolis Club. The Club was organized in 1883 and is one of the places in America where the rich and powerful eat dinner together and talk about how they will continue to rule the world. This is the kind of place where people like George Soros, the multi-billionaire investment guru, gives speeches to private audiences on how the president of the United States is mismanaging one war or another.

The vine covered and sophisticated façade of the Minneapolis Club was built in 1908. The façade of the club speaks to sophistication, wealth, age – maybe even wisdom. But, as I have been noticing, the Club is now surrounded by modern office buildings and stores. One glimpse at the older brick façade is like watching a well dressed aristocrat in a hand-tailored wool suit mingling with younger men clad in polyester. The building no longer belongs here and I wonder if I am also out of place inside this dining room.

Do I really belong inside this Club? Do I really belong at this table, fraternizing with these individuals, in this mahogany clad room, in this exclusive gathering place that was built for the Pretty People? Or, am I just an impostor? Was that the thought in the waitress's mind when she smiled at me with a questioning look? Did she know that I came from a neighborhood more like hers, a neighborhood with no limousines, no Rolls Royce, no private chauffeurs?

I am shocked out of my daydream by the sound of shattering glass. The sound escaped through the doors that protect our dining area from the unsightly kitchen, which is hidden just a few yards away but is designed to feel like it is on the other side of world.

The Pretty People that sit at these tables are not supposed to hear sounds from the kitchen – not in this dining room! The sound of shattering glass propels me back to a painful memory; a memory that violently collides with my upright and respectable relationships with these people. My mind travels back in time…

* * *

Newton Street. Denver, Colorado. My body is filled with adrenaline and I'm running at a flat out sprint across the pavement. I am seething with anger and both of my lips are busted wide open. With each jolting stride the blood from my lips runs down my chin and my shirt takes on the distinct hue of bright red.

As I run around a corner, I can see John's Ford Falcon station wagon through my tear-filled eyes. My step father's prized vehicle is glistening like a bull's eye on a giant target. As I get closer, I see an old brick lying in the grass nearby. I stop briefly to pick it up, tugging it violently from the mud and grass. With the cold brick in my hand, I take several steps and wind my arm back. My muscles are tight and trembling, and I hope that I can aim.

In an attempt to release my wrath, I hurl the brick at the rear side window of the Falcon. During a moment of temporary defeat, the brick bounces off the window in obstinate defiance. Now the brick is also my enemy; the brick, the station wagon, the nearby house, and John, who is in the house. The house represents so much pain. I feel like I owe it something, like the damage I'm about to inflict has a reason and a definite purpose. At that moment, I am a blind warrior. I am my own deliverer. Everyone else has failed me and only I can conquer the storm and overcome the terrors of my life.

The defiance of the brick turns my anger into rage. I snatch the brick off the ground and launch it a second time. The window collapses from the force of my intense agony, and the brick nearly breaks the window on the other side of the Falcon. My brother hears the shattering boom from inside the nearby house, runs out the front door, and screams at me. How could my brother possibly be on John's side? He was there! He saw John's act of violence toward me less than ten minutes ago?

*   *   *

The dinner celebration I am attending at the Minneapolis Club is rolling smoothly along. I take a moment to greet a passing friend, another business leader who has been invited to this celebration dinner. He smiles and shakes my hand. I smile back, but my mind is still thinking about a brick and a window.

I look at the expensive china plate in front of me and at the crystal goblet, filled with purified water, sitting next to the plate. The goblet reminds me of the shattered glass that was just broken in the hidden kitchen nearby, which makes me think again about the shattered glass of John's Ford Falcon station wagon. Sitting at that table in the Minneapolis club, I realize that it was on that fateful day in Denver, years before, that my young teenage mind was also shattered. My mind broke apart like the glass window of the car and like the broken glass in the nearby kitchen. The similarities in sounds are surreal and the memory awakens a terror in my heart. My pulse quickens and I feel a tremor in my hands.

*   *   *

It was September 4th, 1976. I was 13 years old when I threw a brick through the window of the Ford wagon. I should have been home eating breakfast with a nice family or playing baseball at the park. Instead, I was waging a war against the entire world.

When the window shattered, so did my mind. Before its unpleasant introduction to the brick, the Falcon's back window was perfect. I envied the window's flawlessness for my mind was already damaged; it was already permeated with cracks.

Those cracks began forming at a very young age, probably as early as 3 or 4 years old. The story of my childhood is not very uncommon in our broken urban society. It is a story filled with abandonment, broken dreams, abuse, addiction, violence, and an attempt to repress memories. But some memories cannot be repressed. They cannot be repressed because they are recorded in government ledgers, which are designed to measure and weigh people. I was being measured by these government records frequently, and was found wanting. It was as if the records were carefully recording the cracks that were spreading through my mind. By September 4th, 1976, those government records had already recorded many cracks; cracks that represented my budding criminal insanity.

I had been arrested 3 times before I was 10 for shoplifting, but during the 9 months before I threw the brick through the Falcon window, the cracks in my mind were growing rapidly. They seemed to be permeating every corner of my soul. As the cracks grew, the government records grew. During the previous 9 months, I had run away from home 3 times and had been arrested 3 more times, for a total of 6 lifetime arrests. One of the arrests was for smoking pot inside Morey Jr. High School. My most recent school report card also showed signs of my crumbling life. The fact that there was nothing but Fs on that report card, no As, no Bs, no Cs, not even any Ds, was just another physical reflection of the mental breakdown that was occurring.

*   *   *

My mind was very fragile the Saturday morning of September 4th.

The igniting event of that morning was trivial, but forest fires can start with just one spark, and hurricanes with a calm breeze. On that Saturday, dark clouds had already formed, preparing for the hurricane that was ready to break loose. That morning, I woke up in trouble. I had been caught sneaking out the night before with my best friend Kevin Eberl, who had spent the night. When Kevin and I walked up the stairs toward the kitchen, late in the morning, I was prepared for the inevitable hostility that I would face for sneaking out the night before. I was not prepared for what should have been a small disagreement.

By the time I made it upstairs, my brother Kent had completed my Saturday household chores. I am not sure how it is in other families but, in our home, reaching an agreement on how the Saturday chores would be divided was like drafting a treaty between warring nations. It was an agreement driven by compromise – if Kent cleaned the kitchen, I would clean the bathrooms; if Kent vacuumed the living room carpet, I would fold the clothes. Without my permission, Kent and John agreed that Kent would do my Saturday chores and I would do his. I was shocked that Kent and my step-father John had violated all previously established rules for negotiation.

I refused to put up with their crap. How could they make new agreements without consulting me?

"You have to do my jobs today," Kent stated.

"Are you crazy, I never do your jobs," I replied.

"John and I agreed. I did your jobs, now you have to do mine," he proclaimed.

"An agreement between you and John doesn't mean shit to me," I answered.

"You watch your mouth," John said.

"How could you guys decide to switch jobs without talking to me?"

"If you hadn't snuck out last night and woke up on time . . . ," Kent began.

"Well, I don't give a damn about anything that occurred before I woke up." Adrenaline started pumping into my muscles and I was losing control.

Kevin tried to calm me down; he could see the collision coming. "Just cool down and do the jobs, I'll help you."

"You watch your mouth Kip; you are on a short leash today." John said, with increased anger.

"Who are you to boss me around?"

"I'm the one that pays the bills boy, and I have had enough with your mouth."

"Then do something to shut me up. If you think you have control."

Perhaps, if I had been older, more experienced, I would have noticed John's muscles tighten, seen the tight fist and white knuckles. I would have ducked or side-stepped when I saw his arm pull back and shoot forward to meet my unsuspecting lips. I was not prepared when John snapped and punched me dead in the face. I hadn't even seen it coming. Both of my lips were busted wide open and I fell backwards into the wall.

I wish my mother was there that morning. She might have been able to mediate a truce between us. But, as destiny would have it, she was not there when the battle started.

As pain shot into my brain and blood started flowing down my chin, I heard Kevin yell something, but I do not know what. I exploded into a rage. I had had enough of older men beating on me, and I sure wasn't going to take it from an intruding step father. I saw Kent back away as I whipped my head around the room, searching for a weapon. The first thing I could put my hands on was a clock radio, which I catapulted into John's face.

I wanted out of there, to get away from this hateful scene.

"You hit him" Kevin said.

Seeing the shocked look on Kevin's face, I knew I had to get out of there. I yanked the back door open and ran into the yard.

In a state of shock, I started running at full speed. I was looking for something. I was in search of a deep cutting blade of revenge. What could I do to repay his intolerable violation? What could I do to even the score? I thought about John's treasured Falcon station wagon.

I ran around the block to the front of the house. Maybe a little retribution would throttle my anger. But, like most people, when I chose to exercise rage, my anger was not quenched, it was inflamed.

After he heard the breaking glass of the Falcon, Kent bolted outside through the front door of the house to see what I had done. One look at my enraged and bloody face was all it took. He quickly did an about face and ran right back into the house. As a result of our many fights, Kent recognized my state of brutal insanity and decided to get as far away from me as possible.

Because the broken window was insufficient to alleviate my feelings of injury, I ran to the nearest payphone, several blocks away, and called 911 to report the assault.

The lady on the phone replied that the police would not respond. The police responded differently to domestic disputes in those days. In those days, father figures were almost expected to smack their kids around a bit. Keep them in line was the philosophy. But it was not OK with me. In a rising state of abandonment, I told the lady that I would kill John myself. I hung up the phone and started back to the house with revenge on my mind and increased levels of adrenaline pumping into my muscles.

*   *   *

Luckily, my mother intercepted me on a nearby street. She had returned home while I was running to the store. With a brief description of what had occurred, she left the house to look for me.

I don't know how, but she convinced me to get into her car and go for a ride. During the ride, she started to calm me down. It was working well, until I discerned the direction of the discussion. Once I realized what she was doing, my heart sank. All she could talk about was John's injury and the band aid on his nose. She did not seem to care that a grown man had punched her 13 year old son dead in the face. At least, that's how it appeared to me. I felt like I had lost my mother's heart that day and was truly alone in the world.

Taken by themselves, the events of that day should not have been so catastrophic, but they were for me. My heart sank with despondency and my mind shattered. I began an accelerating freefall into darkness. Twelve days later, on Thursday September 16th, I would again run away from my childhood home, but this time I would never return.

My freefall into darkness would bring great trauma. I would experience intense mental pain, debilitating addictions, crippling fear, and extreme self loathing. Part of my descent into gloom would also include frequent interactions with the dark face of death. In fact, all three of the people that were present when John hit me in the face are now dead. Kent and Kevin would die before they were 20 years old and John would end up committing suicide. Kevin was my best friend from my early teens and Kent was my only brother. One of my three step sisters would also die young, before she was 21, and my father would die before I turned 25. I was alone with each of these family members when they died. At the young age of 15, I was alone with my step sister when death took her. Once again, I was alone with my father during his last moments on earth.

When Kent died, it was worse than being alone. We were both surrounded by strangers, not a single familiar face in the crowd. I have learned that the opposite of loneliness is not togetherness. During some of our loneliest moments, we will find ourselves in the midst of strangers. In this case of tragic loneliness, I had to ride with Kent in the back of an ambulance, with strangers. I had to watch, helplessly alone, as unfamiliar faces attempted to bring life back to the dying body of my only brother. After we reached the emergency room, I watched for another grueling two hours as a new set of strangers valiantly attempted to fight death and revive my brother. I was surrounded by strangers, but utterly alone.

My freefall into darkness would bring great trauma and the dark face of death would be my shadow.

* * *

Steve Erickson speaks to me. My mind is jolted back to the Minneapolis Club. Steve, who is sitting across from me at the small dinner table, is the Chief Executive Officer of Datatonix. Datatonix is the technology subsidiary of the Holdings Group. In December 2005, Datatonix had sales of 700 million dollars a year and the Holdings Group had about 50 billion dollars in sales. Steve Erickson is paid millions of dollar a year for leading Datatonix. In a few years, Steve would become the CEO for one of the largest airlines in the world.

Tonight's gathering is small and intimate. A number of the other people in the room also have a "C" at the beginning of their title, like Chief Operating Officer, Chief Technology Officer, Chief Financial Officer, and Chief Marketing Officer. My life has changed so much... I am treated with esteem and admiration by powerful business leaders. Each man shakes my hand and smiles warmly. I am here to receive a coveted award, an award that includes a $10,000 prize. I was given the award to recognize the significant contributions that I have made during the five short months that I have worked for Datatonix.

Karen Fredrich is sitting next to me. Karen is the Director of the Datatonix Innovation Lab. Karen's team is responsible for inventing new products that help solve the healthcare crisis in the United States and the rest of the world. Like most leaders of innovation labs, Karen's mind is sharp and filled with creativity. Karen and I have become friends in the few short months that I have been at Datatonix. I have a simple philosophy when it comes to friends: Accept friendship wherever you find it. Because of my admiration and respect for Karen, I was shocked by what she told me earlier in the day while we were flying to Minneapolis from Salt Lake City.

During that flight, I started to tell Karen about my efforts to write a book. I told her that the book would be about the capacity for human beings to change. I was shocked by her response. It was a response that I have heard from many people, including many of my very educated and intelligent peers. Her words cut my dreams like a knife.

"People do not really change," she said.

If she is right, I am an imposter and I should not be allowed in the Minneapolis Club. If Karen is correct, I do not belong in this mahogany-clad room, drinking from these crystal goblets, eating on this fine china, and fraternizing with these people. If I have not changed, I should be thrown out with the shards of glass from the kitchen.

*   *   *

October 17th 1976. An unknown hour in the morning. Gray skies and a clouded mind. Winter has arrived early in Denver, and today the bitter weather is accompanied by scattered rain. I am waiting for my mother in front of a local convenience store. She is late and I have not seen her since I ran away from home.

Despite the frigid Denver wind blowing in my face, I am sweating. The sweat began when I realized I had agreed to meet my mother in a location with no easy get away. The cops could pull right up and arrest me. Running would be impossible. How could I outrun cops in this open area?

According to the government records that were tracking my criminal behavior, I have been on the run for 31 days. This alone is good reason to wonder if my mother will send the police to capture me.

On October 1st, just 16 days before, my mother had attempted to use the police to catch me. They tried to trap me in the field right behind the same store where I am now standing. As I remember that event, I begin to wonder if I'm making a fool of myself by being here.

The store, Shop n' Go, is located on the corner of Lowell Boulevard and Quincy Avenue in Denver. Behind the store is an open field with a concrete slab from a demolished building. My friends and I spend many hours every day on that slab feeding each other's addictions – smoking pot, drinking alcohol, and doing any other drugs we can get our underage hands on. The naked slab is a fitting place for us to congregate. A decaying old slab is the symbol of our lives; we could have had so much, but instead we have demolished it. Together, hand in hand, we piss and vomit and smash cigarettes on the depressing remnants of our crumbled chances.

Just 16 days ago I barely got away when the cops descended on the slab in an attempt to capture me. Luckily, just after the cops were informed that I was there, I decided to go to the Shop n' Go to get some matches. As I turned the corner to walk to the front of the store, I was shocked to see my mother using the outside payphone. My heart started to pound as my old pal Adrenaline pumped into my blood. My mother never came to this store. Who could she be talking to on the phone? I quickly turned around and bolted back to the slab, jumped into Randy Eberl's Volkswagen van, and begged him to take off.

The van tires kicked up dirt. We were less than 100 yards outside of the field, in the adjoining neighborhood, when we saw the cop car tear into the entrance of the field and shine its blue lights at the bare cement floors of the slab.

Concerned that the cops would start patrolling the surrounding neighborhood, Randy stopped the van, I jumped out, ran to the closest house, and hid behind a bush next to an unfamiliar front door. The cops pulled Randy over less than 2 blocks down the road, but I was no longer in the van. As I was hiding behind the bush, my nerves flared as the front door of the house opened and my brother Kent walked out onto the front porch with a friend. I felt like unseen powers were conspiring against me... again.

Kent obviously had a friend that lived in this very house. What horrible luck. Fortunately, Kent and his friend did not notice me as they proceeded into the yard and disappeared down the street.

Now, like a fool, I am standing in the rain right next to that same payphone that my mother had used to call the police in her last attempt to catch me. I was not sure if I could trust her, but I had been forced to set up this meeting because I had limited options.

As I stand next to the phone, I wonder if my mother will really show up. I decide to wait for her and hope that I will not be greeted by a cop car instead. The sweat pours heavier than the light rain. Just another thing I cannot control.

I am hopeful, because this time I called her and asked for the meeting. I made phone contact two days before and asked my mother if we could talk about a proposal. Who knew what she would think about my "proposal"... I called her because the oldest guy in the apartment where I usually slept had given me an ultimatum: either I had to get a job or I had to go back to school. Otherwise I was useless to him. I think I was like a mirror of his own grizzly failures. He wanted to make an impression on me, get me moving, and keep my sad sack of bones away from his field of vision.

I was not sure who he thought he was, giving me ultimatums, but he did pay the rent and I did not relish the nights when I had to sleep in the cold. Like the night recently when I had fallen asleep under a girl friend's window in a drunken stupor. On that night, while I waited for my girlfriend's mother to go to bed, the power of alcohol had overcome the power of the freezing temperature and caused me to pass out. I woke up in the dead of night convulsing with shivers. My girlfriend did not answer when I lightly knocked on the window. She too must have fallen asleep. I crawled through the unlocked back door of a van in a nearby parking lot and tried to break the shivers, which had escalated to the point of violence.

I experienced some horrible things in my day.

If I did not comply with the older guy's ultimatum to get a job or go to school, I would have to start sleeping in the cold again rather than in his heated apartment. Since I had slept on the streets before, I knew it would be hard for me to go back in the cold of winter.

When I use the description 'heated apartment,' instead of 'warm apartment,' I do so on purpose. Not a person in the world could call that apartment warm. Warmth implies life, it implies security and safety and sanity. The word 'warm' has connotations that do not fit that place.

I was also did not want to leave the heated apartment because both of my friends lived there with me. Doug and Steve were their names. Doug and Steve ran away from home shortly after I did. We were friends because of that common bond.

There were two other guys who also lived in the small apartment. They were in their late teens or early twenties. Their names were unimportant and I would have been hard pressed to remember them, even back then. I was very disconnected from everything. Sometimes I think it was all the drugs. Other times I think it was my collapsing mental state, which may have been helped along by the drugs. Either way, I paid very little attention to anything that didn't concern police, drugs, jail, or the possibility of being thrown into the cold streets.

*   *   *

Speedy Eddie lived across the street from our apartment. He was a skinny ex con who was trying to control his crank habit because of the periodic drug tests administered by his parole officer. I may remember Speedy Eddie for the sole reason that he taught me the art of Short Changing.

Short Changing is a technique you can use to trick convenience store clerks into giving you too much change. Speedy Eddie could reliably turn twenty dollars into twenty three or twenty four through Short Changing. Occasionally, Eddie would Short Change a fifty and get even more. I respected that. A couple dollars wasn't much, but his smooth style gave me something to look up to.

I knew Speedy Eddie would cheat me too if he had a chance, but what could you expect from a strung-out con? New skills like Short Changing helped Doug, Steve, and me support our drug addictions. When we weren't scamming someone or burglarizing houses, we were spending the money on drugs and going to rock concerts. I knew we were screwed when it came to any kind of future, but I didn't care. A retirement plan sounds like a joke to a young teenager with a drug habit. For me, retirement was what I did all day every day. Drugs were my saving grace, as well as concerts and booze.

I had many warnings that I was falling down a dark hole, but I didn't heed them. One night I suffered from alcohol poisoning after a

Tequila drinking contest, but since I didn't die my friends felt that there was no cause for alarm. Another sign, one that hit home a bit harder, was a mental collapse that happened while I struggled to survive a mild overdose of methamphetamine and peyote. I had taken too much of both of these drugs. I vomited everywhere, lost sanity entirely, but overall it was just another night.

*   *   *

Looking up, I could tell the guillotine had been sharpened like a razor. It was waiting to fall, and while I did not care about my neck, I did not want to sleep in the cold, so I called my mom to talk about a way for me to stay in the apartment with Steve and Doug.

I shiver against the wind and rain when finally, coming down the street like a slow motion movie sequence, I see Mom's car. Lucky for me, she's alone.

The walk from the payphone to the car stretched before me. Time and space seem to warp like a nightmare where the thing I want is just ten steps ahead. My feet are heavy; why won't they move? A million thoughts flash through my mind. What is my mother thinking right now? Like specters, demons of shadow, events from my past creep and claw at my memory and I wonder if my mother is haunted by them too.

Is she thinking about the other times when she had to pick me up from a long stretch of trouble? Like the 5 times she had picked me up from police stations or juvenile detention centers? Was she thinking about the time I stole the family vacation money ($300 in 1969), or the time I stole my father's antique coin collection to buy toys, or the time I stole the money my older sister had raised for a charity? Was she remembering the fact that these thefts occurred before I was seven years old? Was she thinking about all the fires I started before I was 8 years old? Was she thinking about the times I stole the family car before I turned 12?

I was mainly worried that she was contemplating the advice she had received from a family counselor. The counselor had warned that kids with my pattern of delinquent behavior at such an early age would spend most of their life in prison, and their life would likely be short and miserable. His opinion: I would not change. Quite a grim individual, the counselor had advised her to let go of me both emotionally and physically.

"Mothers of delinquent criminals are dragged down, beaten, and weathered by the severe consequences of their children's behavior," he said. He straightened his Harvard glasses and adjusted his tie. His hands were firm as they closed the notebook and shook my mother's hand. "Let him go, Mrs. Kreiling, it is the only way for you to find peace."

After all, her mental state had been very fragile. Maybe the family counselor was right. Maybe my bleeding psychological gashes were too deep to heal.

*   *   *

I open the car door and say hello. My mother forces a smile, attempting to conceal her rush of overwhelming helplessness as she looks upon the drug-disfigured body of her baby boy. It is disheartening to look slow death in the face, especially if the slowly dying body is doing the killing to itself. Especially if the body is your son's.

My face shows several weeks of heavy drug and alcohol use and not enough food and certainly not enough sleep. Now a million questions flash through her mind. She asks herself: Where does my son sleep? Does he sleep? What powers have conspired to build the impenetrable wall between me and my little boy? How often does he eat? Does he eat? Why won't he just come home? Where does he wash his clothes? Who sees him when he is not in his clothes? Why does he hate his childhood home so much? Does he brush his teeth? Why was there an extra tinge of coldness in his request to meet with me? What is he thinking? Why has he grown so cold?

We embrace inside the vehicle, but I do not stop sweating. Her suggestion that we go for a drive increases my anxiety. Where will she take me? She suggests that we go for a ride to the mountains near Boulder, Colorado. We had taken many trips to those mountains during better times. My mother is hoping those fond memories will have an influence on our discussion. They don't.

*   *   *

I know I was the source of a lot of pain in my mother's life. I know she does not deserve that pain. But I had become accustomed to pain and accustomed to seeing pain in the lives of those around me. Life is pain.

I force a proposal out of my young mouth that I know will be painful to her.

"I do not want to come home," I say, rubbing my hands together and wiping the beads of sweat from my forehead. "But, I don't want to sleep in the cold." She looks over at me from the driver's seat. "And mom, please take my name off of the All Points Bulletin so the cops will not arrest me for being a runaway.

I'm sick of ducking the cops even when I'm not doing anything wrong. And maybe you could enroll me in school," I say quietly, biting my lip. "My roommates say I have to go to school or they're going to kick me out onto the street."

"You don't have to go to the street!" my mother pleads. "Why don't you understand this? You can come HOME!"

"I can't come home. I don't have a home."

"What? Why not?"

"Look mom: If you can do these simple things I'll do the best I can to make this easy for you. I will go to school, I will earn good grades, I will tell you where I live, and I will visit you once a week for dinner."

Even animals do crazy things when they are cornered. My mother reluctantly agrees, sensing that this is the only way to stay in touch with me.

*   *   *

October 20th, 1976. Three days later. It's my first day at Henry Jr. High. It starts out like most days for an 8th grader. I mat my hair down with water from the sink and brush the dog hair from my shirt. I should have done more to look better, but I woke up late and had to hurry to get to school on time. I leave the apartment without showering or brushing my teeth.

I step over the empty beer cans and broken bottles that line the terrace. In the gusty corner of the staircase, slouched and covered with muddy blankets, is an old man. His nose is swollen purple and he appears to be quite near death. I continue on my way.

It is surprising that Henry Jr. High accepted my enrollment, especially on such short notice. My mother had tried to enroll me here a year ago but they reviewed my behavior record and denied the request.

The previous year I had been attending Morey Jr. High in downtown Denver. Things were going terribly, but at least I was in school. Finally, the ice broke and I was arrested and thrown out for smoking marijuana in the auditorium during an assembly.

"This is a particularly embarrassing incident for the school," the Principal had explained to my crying mother. "Your son is entirely out of control."

Because no other school would accept my transfer, including Henry Jr. High, Morey had to take me back. Morey passed me that year even though I received almost all Fs on my last report card. My grades made no difference. They wanted to get me through the school system as soon as possible. Most of them suspected I was heading for another government system anyway, one with locks, bars, and barbed wire.

Now, less than a year later, Henry Jr. High accepted my enrollment. This is a small triumph in my shattered mind, and as I walk the streets toward the school I feel a strange sense of pride. Henry Jr. High, the school that refused to take me the year before, has recognized my plea. Maybe they suspected that I was at least trying to work within the confines of their dreaded system.

*   *   *

There are girls in the classroom, nicely dressed, mainly smiling. One boy is holding hands with one of the girls and lying to her. I can't tell what he is saying, but I can tell that it's a lie.

I am anxious to tell everyone about my life. How shocked would those little brats be to learn that I was a MAN. I have my own place, my own beers, my own clothes, my own grown-up friends... I was everything that they were not. Even my mother, the iconic figure of discipline and order in a child's life, had no control over me. I was a visionary and I knew the girls would eat it up.

Just then, in the middle of my first class —damn if I know what the class is, who the teacher is, or what she is talking about...—the principal steps inside.

"I need to see Kip Kreiling," he says sternly. The teacher looks helplessly into my eyes, almost as if to say, "Sorry."

The familiar rush of adrenaline fills my body and I begin to panic.

I ask myself, "Who else might be waiting for me in his office?"

I have been to many principal's offices during my short life, but have never been escorted there by the principal himself. I know this is not right – principals never retrieve kids from the classroom.

I stand up and approach him. Smells of perfume, soap, and freshly washed hair intoxicate me as I weave, still hung-over, through the aisles of desks and beautiful people.

The principal is a large man, as many principals are. I imagine that he was probably an athletic coach before becoming a principal. He can probably run very fast. I begin to contemplate: How fast can this jerk really go...?

As we walk out of the classroom into the hall, he purposely positions himself on the left side. The doors to the outside world are on that side of the hall. His positioning is no accident, as he blocks my access to freedom. He is also walking slightly behind me, just like a cop. As I slow down, so does he.

I think about making conversation, but we are separated by a canyon of social differences. It's like the dog catcher and the dog; if only they could talk it out, there would hardly ever be a need for the catch-pole.

Our shoes strike the floor and each step beats like a drum in my chest. We do not exchange a single word. The hall seems to stretch further than normal and my stomach churns. It is the longest five minutes of my life. When I enter the principal's office my fears are confirmed: A glittering badge is waiting for me. His arms are crossed, and when he sees me he reaches for his belt. He handcuffs me and takes me to jail.

This is my 6th arrest, and the second time I have been taken out of a school in handcuffs in less than one year. It's a sad world: My own mother and the school system have conspired to capture me. They'd rather see me in jail than in school. It says something to me about the education system and the intelligence level of our so-called "mentors" and "teachers."

I see the ambush-arrest as deceptive. This view does not improve my trust in adults or authority. I was shocked and couldn't believe how naïve I'd been. No wonder they were so eager to accept me back at Henry Jr. High! No wonder my mother hadn't tried to turn me over to the police on our ride! It was all a ruse! An elaborate attempt to walk me into an even better trap—a foolproof entanglement of nets and barbed wire.

I had learned something from this mistake, and from the whole series of mistakes that had landed me in the back seat of a cop car (which, by the way, is one of the most purposefully uncomfortable places on Earth). I knew not to trust my mother anymore. I knew not to trust the schools. In fact, I now knew not to trust a single human being on the planet.

It was a slow process, but they were helping me succeed: They were turning me into an even harder criminal than I already was.

*   *   *

They lock me up in Colorado's major Juvenile Hall, located in the middle of downtown Denver. This Juvenile Hall is like a high security prison for kids. The building was designed to inspire fear. With its cold frame and barred windows, it clearly has no soul. It's eerily similar to the modern day architecture of Minneapolis, only instead of hamster tubes there is barbed wire and locked doors everywhere.

It is a house for the damned—intentionally built to cage rule breakers and addicts. No real human beings exist inside the sparkling razor wire, only the shells of kids, the guts of whom have long since been wringed out by steel rollers. Everywhere you look zombies roam the barren yards. Staggering young boys grip sharp wire and gaze off at the nearby highway where people drive by on their way to work, soccer camp, cheerleading practice, dinners, movies, dates, family gatherings, or perhaps to rob a bank or buy drugs. The world is filled with billions of people. Sadly, I was one of the ones gripping the barbed wire and waiting.

I had been sent to this Juvenile Hall several months before and recognize one of the kids from my previous incarceration. He doesn't look good. He has a glassy blank stare that he did not have the last time I was here. It was like a couple of months in the gut-wringer had removed years out of this kid's life. The barbed wire had clearly sucked out the gleam of positive anticipation that emanates from the eyes of most boys his age.

This boy has learned the way of this world: cold walls, no colors, echoes, disinfected steel, cold hearts, and the normalcy of a broken mind. This is not the kind of place where a person improves with time. How long

will I be here? Will the same glassy blank stare
penetrate my face in a couple of months? I
believe I am strong willed, but am I strong
enough for this?

As the days pass, I try to adapt to
institutional life. It is good to get regular
meals, but it is mere prison food. We are not
given knives, for obvious reasons (because
we're all "insane" and "crooked" and will
probably stab anyone who comes near us) and
the plastic forks break on the hard waffles.

"Cook told me they've been serving the
same waffles for over two months," a kid tells
me. "They fix a huge batch and then freeze
them. Every morning they take 'em out, put
'em on the hot plate, and there you go." He
smiles, revealing a few missing teeth.

*   *   *

My days are grim in Juvenile Hall. The
tension between the inmates is highest during
gym, where the constant threat of violence
glides above us like birds of prey. When boys
go to gym, the testosterone poison kicks into
high gear, and most of these boys have not
learned to throttle their anger. The nights,
however, are much worse. A sterile locked
room with hollow echoes is terrible for a young
mind, particularly a fractured mind without a
prayer for the future.

What is to become of me? I don't want to go home and I don't know if my mom will even take me now. Is she fully taking the advice of the counselor who advised her to let me go? Is she moving on with her life? How long will I be in this place? How long can my mind, my body, any of it, withstand this unrelenting tension?

As days pass, it becomes clear that some of the kids in my block are part of an outside gang. I try to avoid them, but my luck at dodging a conflict runs its course. One of the kids in the gang says that my cell mate and I are gay. I am not gay, but I have a gay friend in my neighborhood, so I am not completely offended by the accusation.

"You wanna do something about it?" he asks, spitting like some cowboy from a John Wayne movie.

"Don't mess with me," I say. "You don't know who you're up against."

"Yeah I do," he laughs, looking around at all the other fools. This is the only entertainment. The guards turn a blind eye and the argument escalates.

I have enough street smarts to know that the first conflict in jail is the most important one. I learned at an early age that if you make it clear that anyone who screws with you will leave the interaction with pain; you are much more likely to be left alone. Besides, I have been beaten many times by a man and had many fights with Kent, my adopted older brother that had the frame of a Tongan.

I don't wait for any further words. Discussions in jail are like foreplay to a fight. There's no real point in talking if one party can back up his mouth. I jump on the kid and start pounding. It feels good to be in control. For the first time in months everyone is cheering me on. People are screaming, some are kicking us, others are merely laughing and shouting curses from the crowd.

The block guard breaks it up and I am placed in solitary confinement. In solitary, I wonder what will happen when I am released into the open block. I am certainly not looking forward to the next gym session. What will become of me when I am reintroduced into the common population? A quarrel with an established gang member can mean serious injury.

"Will this fight be the short road to the hospital?" I ask myself, staring into the fluorescent light—the sole source of illumination in the solitary cell.

Luckily, I am released from juvenile hall before the solitary confinement period reaches its end. I leave the building hoping that the other kid rots in solitary and forgets all about me. I know he won't forget, but it's a pretty good bet I won't see him again.

*   *   *

My next stop is a foster home. This home is just one more move in what becomes an unending search for a place where I can try to find some sanity. At this time, I have no idea how long that search will take and it is probably good that I do not know. Between the ages of 11 and 26, I will move 34 times; on average, I moved every five months for 15 years.

During that same period of time, my mother only moved three times and my father only moved twice. As an adult, when people ask where I was raised, I stumble in my response and just mutter that I moved a lot. They invariably ask if I was an army brat.

"Yes, I was a brat," I think to myself. "And yes, I was in a war."

I have never really learned how to give an elegant answer to this question. Some questions do not have elegant answers.

The foster home, despite how I loathe the idea, is not that bad. The couple that run the foster home are nice people. They have made arrangements with a 7UP factory for an unlimited supply of short fill bottles of soda (bottles that were not completely filled by the manufacturing equipment). They have also made arrangements for an unlimited supply of day-old donuts from Winchel's Donuts.

The only other kid living in the house is friendly. We make small talk and spend time playing cards or telling stories from our wrecked lives...

The foster parents are also unable to go upstairs, where my room is, because of medical problems. I conclude that this is not such a bad setup: unlimited donuts, soda, nice people, and an opportunity to escape to my bedroom for privacy. I am told that if I am "good" I can return to my mother's home in 6 months. Maybe this place will provide me with an opportunity to figure out some kind of next step in my life.

My first day at the new school arrives, and I'm nervous. I sweat all through my first class; an unbending torment inflicts strange anxiety on my mind. I am breathing heavily, gripping my pencil, staring at the other kids like a rabid wolf, and not listening to a single word from the teacher.

Between classes I go to the bathroom and mill around looking for kids who look like they're cool.

"Hey," I say, eyeing a kid with a dirty jacket and bushy afro. He is growing stubble on his face and it's coming through in patches like dying grass.

"What's up?" he asks, giving me a strange eye and stepping up to the urinal.

"You got any weed? Anything like that? I've been locked up for..." I give him my spiel and he confers with a boy at the door.

The other boy comes over, flashes me a plastic bag, and nods. I offer to trade my watch for whatever is in the bag. I have not been able to get any drugs in juvenile hall or the foster home so I have not had anything for several weeks. He is not impressed by my offer, he wants cash, but I plead with him.

"Lemme see that watch," the boy says.

I hand him the hardware. He quickly slides the plastic bag into his pocket and turns to walk away. My heart starts to pound as I realize he plans on taking my watch. I push him hard. As he starts to lose his balance, I snatch the watch out of his hand and bolt for the bathroom door.

As I slide through the door, I hear his threatening words "We'll be watching for you outside."

I clearly see that I am not going to get along very well in this school; partly because I am one of the few white kids here. I decide that maybe I should give it up. As I trudge down the hall on my way to my next class, I feel a bug rising into my throat.

I don't even want to return to my mother's home. Attending this school is a joke. It's a waste of my time. I contemplate going back to the bathroom and attacking the boy who tried to steal my watch but ponder the fact that there are two of them, maybe more.

I leave the school that day, just walk out one of the side doors, and never return to the foster home. This will be the second school that I will attend for less than one day.

I make it all the way back to my neighborhood, to the naked slab behind the Shop N Go. I take a seat on a piece of cement and close my eyes. I let out a long sigh. Home sweet home…

*　　*　　*

My friends are shocked to see me. Even they are beginning to wonder what is going on in my mind.

Returning to the heated apartment is not an option because I told my mother where it was. With nowhere to go, I leave the slab and wander the grey streets during my first day of "freedom." As evening approaches, I realize I will have to find shelter. The coat I am wearing will provide poor protection from the bitter Denver cold.

My search brings me to the edge of a fallow field. A small grove of trees grows suspiciously in the middle of the field. It looks like a dangerous spot, but I head there anyway. Maybe the branches of the trees will offer some comfort tonight.

As I enter the grove I see that someone has built a crude structure. The previous occupant has stacked three old mattresses like flap-jacks. They are sinking into the muddy ground like maple syrup. The bottom one is soaked completely. The brown, wet stains have worked up the side. On the second mattress I can see a line where the moisture has permeated it as well. Luckily, the top mattress appears to be dry. As I lay down I hope that the mottled stains on its surface are from water and not the bodily fluids of some derelict.

I peer up at the sky, peeking between the slats of the roof and try to wrap my coat around me tighter, to drive the chill away. I try to sleep. Sometime in the night, with my teeth chattering, I nod off, neither knowing or caring what may happen the next day.

The next morning I am awakened by some kids peering into my new home, probably on their way to the nearby school. After they wake me up I try to talk to them, but they run away. Of course they run away. What do I have to offer anyone? I bet they never guess that the person calling after them is just a little older than they are. During the next day or two, I acquire a sleeping bag from somewhere and decide to make this structure my nighttime home. I also try to bring order to my life. But the order follows my previous pattern: stealing and searching for drugs. Most mornings I get up, wrap my sleeping bag around me to stay warm, and go meet Doug and Steve. I usually walk through the parking lot of the Shop n Go, where I met my mother several weeks before.

One day, while walking through that parking lot, a familiar car pulls up to the gas pump. My sister Kay and her husband Dave are inside the car.

"Dave, do you recognize that boy?"

I can't hear anything through the closed windows of the car, but I duck my head down slightly and try to scurry through the parking lot without being noticed.

"I can't tell for sure," Dave says, "what do you think?"

I do not know what they will do and I really do not want them to see me in this condition. My long hair has not been combed this morning and I have not recovered from the drugs and alcohol of the night before.

Kay recognizes my walk.

"Oh, my God, I think that's my brother."

Dave jumps out of the car and yells my name.

As I turn to look at him, tears well up in my eyes when I see the compassionate look on his face.

They take me to their home and give me some much needed food. They wonder what to do with me, knowing that I do not want to go home and that I will probably not stay in another foster home. They take the path of moral courage and invite me to live with them.

I only live there for three or four months, but I fill those months with trauma. They should have known what to expect. I gave them fair warning. They said that I could sleep in their unfinished basement, that we could create a private area by hanging up some curtains. They offered me their old king-sized water bed to sleep in.

My response was cold. "I will not live with you unless you let me smoke pot in the basement."

They agreed to my ridiculous demand, even though they were raising young children in the house. They agreed in a futile attempt to reach my shattered mind. I had clearly fallen several hundred feet further down a very dark hole and they were trying to throw me a lifeline.

Just four or five weeks before, I complied with an ultimatum that caused me to call my mother so that I would not have to sleep in the cold. Now, I preferred living in a hobo-built shanty rather than agree to any terms that would separate me from my drug habits. My perceived "freedom" was wrecking my ability to survive. I had an insatiable hunger for illicit, illegal, mind-altering, and life-changing experiences. I was drawn to things that would wreak havoc on my world. My choices were unexplainable and dangerous, but these choices were my freedom and this lifestyle was my path.

*   *   *

Some of the trauma that I caused during those few months was relatively mild. Like the day I blew my thumb nail off while playing with fireworks in a nearby field – the same field where I would do drugs with my friends at the naked slab. This was the kind of distress you expected from a hyper-active 13 year old boy and this was something that my family was used to.

But trauma seemed to be my trademark – trauma of a dark hue. I had the power to bring misery to simple activities. For instance, one night when Dave, Kay, and I tried to play a simple game of Monopoly I lost my cool.

I knew that Dave almost always won Monopoly, but tonight I am beating him handily.

"Looks like you've lost your smarts," I say to Dave.

He shrugs my aggressive comment off and hands me a few blue bills.

"I thought smoking pot made a person stupid?" I joked. "How is it that I'm beating you? I'm stoned out of my mind right now!" I laughed and looked at Kay. She was not smiling.

Out of nowhere, Dave slapped me in the face. I seemed to have developed a skill for evoking anger in others. My sister's volcanic reaction toward Dave is probably the result of our upbringing. My sister and I were raised in a violent home.

"I can't believe you would smack a kid like that," Kay says. "It's not right."

"He pissed me off, Kay. He was purposely provoking me. He was asking for it."

"So it's OK to slap someone?" she asks.

"Yeah, if they make you mad enough."

Based on Dave's last statement, I drew back my arm and nailed him, open palm, in the face. Fortunately, that slap made Dave realize what he had started. He pins me to the floor and playfully thumps my chest a couple of times.

"GUYS!" Kay yells. "Stop screwing around!"

Dave attempts to turn the fight into a playful wrestling match. It does not work. I struggle free, run out the door, jump onto my stolen mini motorcycle and drive to the nearby field. Unable to control my emotions, I begin to weep.

Dave finds me, tears filling his own eyes.

"I'm sorry," he says. "It's just that we're so similar." He's trying to build a bond between us. I can recognize what he's doing, but I think it's nice of him. It's touching. No one ever wants to make a bond with me.

"It's alright," I say.

"Why don't you come back to the pad? We'll just hang out. No more Monopoly."

We both chuckle and he helps me to my feet. I am not used to compassionate apologies from adults. But, even through his compassion, I remember that Dave has reasons to feel real anger toward me. I have brought much bigger traumas into their peaceful home during these months. Like the disturbance brought by the unexpected visitors who arrived within a week after I moved into their apartment...

*   *   *

There was a loud knock on the front door. The blue uniforms filled up the doorway and Dave stood there baffled.

"Can I help you guys?"

"Is this your residence, sir?"

"Yeah," Dave said, shrugging his shoulders. The Denver breeze swept into the house, rousing Kay from the kitchen. She peered into the living room.

"Your name?"

As soon as Dave gave them his name, they spun him around and handcuffed him – right in front of his wife and children!

"You are under arrest for the transportation of stolen goods," the cops said. They recited the license plate number of his vehicle. Following a brief interrogation, they figured out that the crime had been perpetrated by someone else, but someone using Dave's car. Dave called me up from the basement and I was arrested again.

This time I was arrested for burglary, which the city viewed as contemptible beyond my usual vagrancy and substance violations. This time, they took finger prints. This time, they took mug shots. This time, they really wanted to keep track of me. Another record was created.

"On or about the 25th day of November, A.D 1976, at the City of Lakewood, County of Jefferson, DANIEL KIPLING KREILING, did unlawfully, feloniously and knowingly break an entrance into and enter and remain unlawfully in the dwelling and occupied structure of Erma J. Staffen . . . with the intent to commit therein the crime of burglary second degree; . . . and against the peace and dignity of the People of the State of Colorado."

Of all days, I had committed this crime on Thanksgiving Day. On that Thanksgiving Day, while most people were thankful for good food and family, I was out on the streets like a stray dog. For a guy like me, Thanksgiving Day meant being thankful for acquiring Erma J. Staffen's stuff. These were certainly very strange days, and the police officers took turns shaking their heads in outright disgust.

*   *   *

I was arrested two more times while living with Dave and Kay. One of the additional arrests was also for burglary. In the other arrest, I was taken out of a bank in

51

handcuffs because I started a fight with the security guard. I was slightly drunk. I somehow presumed that the security guard was insulting me, so I initiated the brawl.

"It's embarrassing," Kay told me. "It's... unreal."

The shock of my behavior was setting in. At points, while scolding me, family members would chuckle and raise their arms in question. Laughter is a common response when an individual is unable to believe something they're hearing. I guess I was just "unbelievable."

* * *

Dave and Kay decided to move into a smaller home. There was no longer room for the boy with the shattered mind. I moved on, like a locust, to devastate others.

As my destructive behaviors continued, so did the cracks in my mind and the government records of those cracks. By the time I reached 16, I was arrested 13 times.

I began dealing drugs and organizing small-scale criminal operations. I owned and carried several hand guns, and I shared a home with a strip dancer who worked at a club called Lucifer's Follies. I thought my living situation was hilariously fitting.

I also moved in and out of many addictions. At various times, I was heavily addicted to cigarettes, alcohol, marijuana, methamphetamine, cocaine, and other street drugs. I had also used LSD, mescaline, MDA, peyote, mushrooms, and other hallucinogenic substances.

Unlike many users, I wasn't interested in the science behind drugs. I still don't know the composition of some of the drugs. Many times I would take a drug on the spur of the moment, often without asking what it was or how much of it I should take.

This carelessness led to several drug overdoses, including one in which I may have experienced clinical death. Maybe the family counselor was right. Maybe my bleeding psychological gashes were too deep to ever heal. Maybe I would spend a short and miserable life in prison. Or maybe I would die. At this point in time, change seemed impossible.

* * *

The Minneapolis Club. December 2005. I am looking at Karen Fredrich, who is still sitting next to me.

"People never change," she had said on the plane. A vision of her face, those painful words, plays in a realistic daydream.

Is she right? Is change impossible?

The waitress walks across the room. Is my interpretation of her smile correct? Am I an imposter? Do I belong in this club? Do I belong with these people?

I know that I am not an imposter. In fact, I have completely changed. I am more like the people that I am having dinner with in the Minneapolis Club than I am the juvenile criminal that robbed Erma J. Staffen's home on Thanksgiving Day. When I meet new people today, unless I tell them my history, none of them would ever know that I was a juvenile drug addict and hardened criminal.

Following my changes, I have witnessed and contributed to dramatic changes in the lives of hundreds of people. As a business professional, I am a turn-around expert – I help companies fix broken projects, broken initiatives, and broken divisions. On the high end, I have contributed to business turnarounds for companies that generate almost $10 billion in annual sales.

Through my own transformation and the other changes that I have helped with, I have discovered eight principles, which, when practiced, can lead to a more abundant life.

The focus of this book is to share those discoveries so that you can transform yourself, your marriage, your family, your businesses, your community, and your world. I hope that these discoveries lead to dramatic and positive changes in your life, as they have in mine.

This is, in fact, one of my greatest ambitions, one of my greatest hopes, one of my greatest dreams, and one of my most sincere prayers. Whenever you embark on a journey of personal or organizational transformation remember this important First Principle:

Principle #1: You can completely change.

How this book is structured:

Because this book is more of a guide for describing the eight principles of transformations than it is a memoir, the following chapters are focused on these key principles and how these principles helped me change my life. To achieve this objective, the chapters are structured based on the logical order of those principles, versus the chronological order of the events in my life. I call the next principle Burning Boats.

CHAPTER TWO

BURNING BOATS

Am I dead? I watch from above as my abused body lay motionless on the shoddy bed below me. My mind does not want to face the truth that is right in front of me, so it focuses on the trivial details surrounding my body. How cheap the paneling looks. Old and dirty, the paneling is too close to my bed. The carpet is stained and ratty. The sheets, the blanket, the pillow case, have gone too long without being washed.

Before seeing my body on the bed, I was already in a state of severe mental distress. Looking down from the ceiling, as though I was hung up there on a clothes line, I become even more confused and troubled. I am no longer in my body. How can I see it? What am I using for eyes?

If my body is on the bed, how can I be hovering above it? Why does the ceiling suddenly appear to be so far above the bed? Does some other world exist above the ceiling? Why does the distance seem to be growing? Are the dreadful events of the last several hours over? Am I dead? More importantly, do I deserve to die? If I do not deserve to die, can I find a path back to the physical world that appears to be right in front of me?

I can see my body and I desperately claw at the space between us. I need to regain my composure. Floating in space is unreal, a terrible punishment bestowed upon me as a result of my uncontrollable drug habit.

*   *   *

In early January 1980, I had an out-of-body experience. I do not know if I experienced clinical death, but I am sure that I was knocking on the door of another dimension, maybe even the next world. This is the story of the events that led to that horrific night and to a concept I now call Burning Boats.

Similar to other horrifying occurrences in my youth, the events of this night were the result of several poor decisions.

It all started with a robbery. In this case, I was the victim. I was robbed of several hundred dollars, which, in 1979 in Augusta, Georgia, was a lot of money. At least, it was a lot of money for a 16 year old kid like me. To make matters worse, the money that was stolen was not mine. The cash belonged to Randy, my primary drug dealer.

I had been dealing drugs for several years, but now it was my primary source of income. Like most of the characters that dealt in large quantities of drugs, Randy was a little crazy. Randy was also connected to organized crime. I aspired to gain his connections and take my business to the top level. I had a long way to go.

Like many of my associates in those days, Randy carried guns. Not only was he packing heat, he was not afraid to pull it out and spray hot lead all over the Augusta streets. Despite the danger, I worked exclusively with Randy because he had the best coke, which I was taking more and more frequently, almost every day. Now, with Randy's money in the hands of another street punk, I knew our relationship would be over. He may even decide to pull his gun on me. Who knew what he would do?

I was paranoid, on the edge of my wits. The cocaine had snapped my mind into a state of uncontrollable suspicion. I shuffled down the streets and whispered plans into the night.

"I can go over to Kim's..." I mumbled, jumping at the shadow of a stray cat in the alleyway. "She's not friends with Randy. Maybe Randy won't ever find me over there..."

I snuck back to my home, hoping to avoid Randy, jumped into my car, and drove over to Kim's. She agreed that I could stay at her place while I saved up the money to pay Randy back.

Like many other members of my family, Kim had had a hard life. The father of her two children had died in a motorcycle accident when the kids were very young. Fortunately, a small insurance settlement helped her pay the bills, but there was not enough money to live in comfort. Kim was forced to live in a very low-end trailer park – not the kind of trailer park with doublewide trailers, cement driveways, wood verandas, big bedrooms, or real-wood paneling. She and her kids were barely getting by. But, you cannot mistake the look of the home for the size of the heart. She welcomed me into her home despite my appearance. My coke addiction had taken its toll. Anyone could see it: The dark circles under my eyes, the nervousness, the paranoid twitches. Despite my ragged and coked-out appearance, Kim had no problem with me hanging out at her place until I could get back on my feet.

There were two options, and I would take whichever came first. I either needed to get the money to pay Randy, or I needed to find a new connection to replace him. The drug business was booming, and if I took too long to get another supply, my customers would move on as well. I was hopeful that Kim's next door neighbor, Rocky, would be able to help me pay Randy back or restore my business and gangster reputation.

In keeping with the general tone of the trailer park, Rocky had had a hard life. I did not know a lot about him, but his most obvious challenges appeared to be the direct result of using hard drugs; heroin, specifically.

In one of Rocky's drug induced stupors, he wandered onto a road and was hit by a car. This accident had permanently disabled him, leaving him with a severe limp. Rocky also had another sign of a relentless drug addiction. The swollen flesh, the bruises, several veins in his arms had collapsed from too many needle injections. It was pitiful the way he limped around, the way his scarred arms hung down like dead tree branches. It was pathetic, but he was just the kind of guy I needed to befriend.

Rocky claimed to have connections with the Syndicate, which was an organized drug ring in Georgia. He claimed that he was going to get a shipment of a new drug called Rocket Fuel. According to Rocky, NASA had developed a new compound to propel rockets. A derivative of this new compound had the unintended "benefit" of being a very potent street drug. I had never heard of such a drug, before or since, but I needed a new drug supply, and this just might be it.

Hoping that Rocky was the answer to my dilemma; I would go to his trailer every day.

Knock, knock.

"What is it, kid?" He'd approach the door, peer out into the Georgia sun.

"How about that Rocket Fuel?"

"Hasn't come in yet. I told you kid, I'll let you know when it does."

"How much longer?" I asked, knowing that the Fuel was my ticket to paying Randy.

"I said I'll come find you."

Day after day I would go to Rocky's trailer and I would leave in disappointment. Eventually, I stopped going. Rocket Fuel... how stupid could I be! There was no such thing! This junkie had been leading me on, playing me for a fool.

Rocky showed up late on a Sunday night. It was late enough that everyone in the trailer had already gone to bed – the lights were off, the stars were out, and the crickets were chirping. The pounding on the front door woke me up. I let Rocky inside.

"What do you want this late at night?" I asked.

"Hey kid," he muttered, obviously high on something.

"What's going on?" I whispered, not wanting to wake Kim or the kids.

"Check me out." He pulled out a bag from his pocket.

I literally ran into my bedroom and grabbed a mirror and razor blade. I rolled a dollar bill into a makeshift snorting straw while Rocky placed some of the Rocket Fuel powder on the mirror. I used the razor blade to arrange the powder on the mirror into a line and then snorted the powder up my nose. That's how the Rocket Fuel began its journey into my mind: I snorted it into my nose, it penetrated my nasal membranes, seeped into my blood stream, flowed through my veins, and blasted right into my brain. I quickly found out what it was like to have Rocket Fuel in my brain.

"It takes a minute," Rocky said, leaning back on the worn-out coach.

"You wanna see my new piece?" I asked.

"Sure."

I pulled out my loaded Saturday Night Special from beneath the cushion of the nearby easy chair. He took it in his hand and pointed it at the wall.

"Pretty nice."

"Thanks," I said, shoving it back into the hiding spot.

Carrying a gun was just one of the gangster-like habits that I had adopted. These habits hid the changes that were occurring in my heart. I was changing in positive ways but nasty habits die hard, and my gangster-like habits effectively hid any positive changes that the world might have noticed.

Consequently, the fact that I was already deep into a positive transformation was not apparent to most people. I had recently started to ponder the effects that hard drugs were having on my body and mind. In fact, I was seriously entertaining the idea of giving up hard drugs altogether. Even though those thoughts were positive, this was probably not the best time to expose them to Rocky.

"I'm quitting hard drugs," I said.

"What!" Only those who have been heavily addicted to hard drugs could fully relate to Rocky's emotional response. I understood it. Some of these drugs pull you into a world in which you cannot see, or even desire, anything else. Some of these drugs can own your mind, and worse, they can own your heart.

"Drugs are ruining my body, man. I look in the mirror and I can't even recognize myself anymore."

"What are you talking about? Drugs don't do a damn thing to your body!"

The scars on Rocky's arms glared up at me. The Rocket Fuel was affecting my brain. I could feel myself falling off a cliff.

"Look at your arms," I said woozily.

"What are you talking about?"

"You're arms, man. All the veins are collapsed. You used the needle too much."

"You better watch it, kid."

"I'm sorry, man, I'm just... ripped..."

"You can't be THAT high, it hasn't had time to take effect yet." He laughed.

Rocky, with a vengeful look in his eyes, asked me if I wanted more.

"You want another line?"

I was a tough guy. I prided myself on the quantity and variety of drugs I could take. I had started using pot at 10. I took LSD, peyote, and multiple other hard drugs at 12 and 13. One of the shocking aspects of my early drug experience was the fact that I had never hallucinated, even on LSD, at the young age of 12! I took pride in the fact that I had a high tolerance for drugs and foolishly believed that it was an indication that I had a strong mind. I still do not know what I truly meant by my absurd belief that I had a strong mind, but I believed it nonetheless.

Because of this absurd belief, I rarely said no to "more." I wanted more.

"Gimme another line" I said.

Rocky dumped another big, fat line on the snorting mirror on the coffee table in front of me.

I should have realized that the line was too big.

"Rocket Fuel," I said. We laughed.

I had not given the first dose enough time to have its full effect when I leaned down and snorted the second line into my nose, off the mirror. While the mind-altering effects of the first dose were still increasing, the second dose penetrated my nose membrane, seeped into my veins, and blasted into my brain. The combination of the escalating impact of the first dose and the blast of the second one took my mind over the edge of sanity. I, even with my "strong mind," started my first hallucination. For some experiences in life, the first one is not the best.

While Rocky was sitting on the nearby couch, I was sitting in the easy chair in the center of the room. With the thought of Rocket Fuel on my mind, and with Rocket Fuel actually coursing through my brain, the term Rocket Fuel made me think of Captain Kirk, from Star Trek. For many years I had watched Star Trek, wasted on one drug or another. Tonight I would pay for that little diversion. Suddenly, I WAS Captain Kirk. Suddenly, I was sitting in Captain Kirk's chair on the deck of the Starship Enterprise.

The starship took off into space. At this point, the hallucination began digressing from the Star Trek storyline. Instead of the Enterprise gracefully taking off from a space station, the hull of the ship trembled and roared, to the point where I assumed it would collapse. I sunk my finger nails into the arm rest of the easy chair and pressed my feet against the floor in an attempt to steady myself. The rocket engines, apparently strapped to the side of the trailer, with full sound and severe shaking, blasted the fragile rectangle box into the sky.

As the stars rushed by the nearby window, I remembered my absurd belief that I had a strong mind. As I was blasting into space in a trailer, I remembered that I had never hallucinated before. Knowing that I was now hallucinating and that I had just taken the second line of Rocket Fuel moments before, I knew I was screwed – SCREWED!!!

In the darkness of space, a very dangerous voice began to dominate my thinking.

"Rocky overdosed you on purpose," the voice said. "You should have never opened your mouth about his veins."

The ship continued to rise through the sky and my mind shook in fear and breathtaking anxiety.

"You are going to die," the voice told me. A sense of despair welled up in my heart. "Get the gun from under the chair. Kill Rocky. You are doomed, at least take him out before you die. Rocky killed you. Kill Rocky."

As thoughts of revenge began to close my mind somehow my compassionate and reasonable side broke through. Suddenly the rocket hallucination stopped and we were back on the ground. I was concerned that the dangerous voice would return, so I commanded Rocky to leave the trailer. Commanded is the right word. Even in the haze of the moment, Rocky recognized the reason behind the command. Rocky recognized the danger. I was on the verge of violence and he was the target. He immediately stood up and started to leave. As Rocky stood up, I must have also stood up because the last thing I remember before I stumbled into my nearby bedroom was watching Rocky leave the trailer.

"Hurry up," I slurred. "And keep your distance from that easy chair."

Breaking my established habit, I stumbled into my small bedroom without my gun, which was still hidden under the easy chair. Perhaps I knew that a gun was not going to protect me from the coming ordeal. The next 7-8 hours were beyond any nightmare I had ever imagined and, because my cousin and her young children were fast asleep, it was a nightmare that I would experience alone. There is nothing quite as terrible as a hallucinogenic overdose in the middle of the night, especially in a home where no one has any idea that you are dying, that your mind is collapsing, that you have left the confines of Earth and are traveling to terrifying places that do not seem real.

I have many fleeting memories of the experiences of that night, and cannot clearly recall the exact order in which they occurred, but I will do my best to describe them. The most vivid memory was the tumult that was occurring inside my body. It felt like an energy of some kind was reverberating from my head, through my body tissue, to my toes, where it seemed to bounce off of my toes and reverberate back to my head, where it bounced again and headed back to my toes – back and forth, back and forth, back and forth, back and forth. This force also felt like it moved in a physical wave, like waves were passing through my body tissue – back and forth, back and forth, back and forth, back and forth. These waves felt like the waves of the sea, violently and incessantly beating the shore.

When the energy force passed through my head, it made a "VVUU" sound. At first the energy moved very fast, with the incessant "VVUU, VVUU, VVUU, VVUU," as the waves passed very quickly through my head. This went on for hours. While the energy was bouncing back and forth between my head and toes, my entire body was shaking inside, like an earthquake – shake, shake, shake, shake, shake. I remember wondering how a wave could pass back and forth through tissue that was already violently shaking.

When I described this experience to a doctor, many years later, he said I probably experienced a prolonged seizure. How comforting.

Another vivid memory I have was a flock of birds. A small tree was positioned directly outside the window of my room of the trailer, and my bed was right next to the window. I remember believing that the small tree was full of hundreds of birds, which were all tweaking – "Tweak, tweak, tweak, tweak, tweak!"

I later recalled friends achieving a drug induced state that they called Tweaking. I sure hoped this was not the state they referred to. This was a state I never wanted to encounter again – tweak, tweak, tweak, tweak, tweak.

*   *   *

At some point during this nightmare, my mind was no longer in my body, but was floating at the top of the room, looking down at my body. My mind, my soul, my spirit, something separate and distinct from my body had separated itself and flown away.

I cannot remember when this occurred during the multi-hour torment. I do remember looking down from the ceiling and being surprised that my body was not shaking or moving at all. I am not sure if the seizures stopped when my spirit was outside of my body, or if they were not actual seizures.

Unfortunately, the out-of-body experience was not the most horrifying part of this ordeal. The most traumatizing experience occurred when I was back in my body. The trauma arose from the contradictory paralysis. Contradictory because, while my body was experiencing the internal earthquakes and the reverberating waves, I could not move and I could not speak. No matter how hard I tried, I couldn't utter a word. I could not move and I could not speak!!! I remember thinking I would yell for help, if only I could.

An overwhelming fear filled my soul. The energy, bouncing from my head to my toe, with the accompanying "VVUU, VVUU" sound, began to slow down. I could foresee a point in which the energy, with the accompanying internal earthquakes and waves, would stop. The overwhelming fear arose from the fact that I could not move and I could not speak. I knew I was back in my body, I could no longer see my body from the ceiling, but what was the condition of that body? I had visions of living as a human vegetable – able to see the world and hear the sounds around me, but unable to move or speak. This fear overcame me and my mind began to sink into greater despair.

My descent into greater darkness was unexpectedly halted by a comforting voice that spoke hope to me. In response, I started a dialogue with some being from the unseen world. A dialogue, not with my mouth, but spoken in my mind and soul. I later believed that I spoke to God, but I do not know for sure. What I do know is that I perceived that this being had the power to restore my life. This was the message of hope. With this encouraging realization, I began to beg that I would be restored to full health.

Even in this desperate state, I recalled seeing movies in which the leading character bargained with God for his life. I did not believe in bargaining with God, even though I was not raised in a particularly religious home. If there was such a being, surely we should approach him or her with humility, not with bargains. My current state changed that perspective. I begged for my life, and I started to bargain.

"Please restore my body to full health and I promise I will stop using hard drugs! Forgive me for the way I have treated the precious gift of life! Please, please save me from the paralysis that is preventing me from moving or speaking! If you save me, I will not only stop using hard drugs, I will stop smoking cigarettes and I will stop drinking alcohol! Please have mercy on my soul!" I was on the edge of my sanity. I continued to do what any normal person would do: I begged for my life.

Miraculously, at least to me, I was rescued.

*   *   *

This is not intended to be a religious book. This is a book about transformations of multiple types, personal and professional alike.

Not having any religious convictions at this time, I did not expect this experience, but it happened to me.

I spoke with a being from the unseen world, and my pleas were granted. Shortly after the dialogue with this personage, I could move and I could speak. About that time, I noticed that the sun was rising outside my bedroom window, and the birds were no longer tweaking in the nearby tree.

On that new day, because of the terror, pleas, and bargains from the night before, I kept my promise. I stopped using hard drugs, tobacco, and alcohol. Even though I had smoked cigarettes from the age of 10, and smoked over a pack a day at this time, I stopped smoking – cold turkey. Even though I had developed an alcohol addiction by age 11, and even though alcohol was inextricably intertwined with my current social life, I stopped drinking – cold turkey. I had made a deal with God, had spoken to Him directly, and I was going to keep my word.

*   *   *

What does this experience have to do with transformations and burning boats? My life has completely changed from my days as a juvenile criminal. Today, I am a business executive and I am often asked to work on transformations for very large companies. Outside of my paid job, I teach personal transformation classes and have helped many friends, new and old, overcome obstacles in their lives and achieve their dreams. Through the many business and personal transformations that I have been part of, I have learned this important lesson: Major transformations will not occur until the transformation becomes an imperative. This is the central message of this chapter.

Again, major transformations will not occur until the transformation becomes an imperative.

An imperative is a necessity, a compelling need, an overwhelming desire. In simple terms, an imperative is something that we are compelled to do. Major transformations will not occur until the transformation becomes a necessity, a compelling need, and an overwhelming desire. Unfortunately, for me it took a near death experience to break my teenage dependency on hard drugs, cigarettes, and alcohol. My overdose on Rocket Fuel helped me reach the point where giving up these addictions became a necessity for my survival.

Human beings are creatures of habit. As a whole, we hate change. Most of us follow the saying, "If it's not broke, don't fix it." This approach often allows us to coast through life without too much trouble.

For those of us who spend our working hours trying to bring about corporate or organizational changes, and personal ones, we run into this "anti-change" obstacle every time. People will tenaciously hold on to very bad habits, because they hate to change. People are stubborn.

Why is this so? For most of us, the fear of loss is much stronger than the desire for gain. This fear is a highly emotional trait, rather than a logical one. Many of us can logically see changes that need to occur, in our personal lives, in our families, in our jobs, but we are unwilling to change. This is just simply how we are wired.

When we encounter this emotional barrier, we can be fooled by the mistaken belief that resistance to change is caused by the age of the organization or by the age of the workers – that older organizations and older workers are the ones who will not change. This is often untrue. I have had many experiences that demonstrate the fear of change is not limited to older organizations or people. One of these experiences was in the Home Products Division of Hewlett Packard (HP).

The Home Products Division (HPD) designed, produced, and sold the award-winning Pavilion Personal Computer. HPD was a unique division at HP. It was purposely set up with a charter that allowed the division to bypass many of the rules and tedious processes that other HP organizations had to follow.

HP had made several previous attempts to compete in the very competitive personal computer market but those attempts had failed. An analysis of those failures was conducted. HP had one of the best names in the computer business. Focus group after focus group confirmed that US consumers associated HP with innovation, quality, and compassion. But HP continued to fail in the personal computer marketplace.

How could it fail so often when HP was a recognized technology leader with such a positive image? The analysis of those previous failures answered the question. HP's normal decision making process was too slow to respond to the rapidly changing personal computer market. HP's positive culture was partially built on a consensus decision style, which meant that many people had to be consulted and often had to agree with decisions before any changes could take place. This process was simply too slow.

To respond to this organizational challenge, HP setup the Home Product Division allowed that division to operate with very high levels of autonomy. HPD could by-pass much of the red tape that other divisions had to comply with. The division was also staffed with very young people, partly because the leadership believed that younger people can respond to rapidly changing environments and because it was a very exciting opportunity. In a division that was setup and staffed to be flexible, with young employees, I was asked to help lead a small project.

My project group was asked to improve the process used to communicate purchase prices for computer components. We had one team that flew around the globe negotiating purchase prices for computer components like hard drives, key boards, floppy drives, monitors, etc. We had another team that created the purchase orders to buy those components. The problem: The team responsible for creating the purchase orders often did not know that the other team had negotiated a new price for a specific component. Not knowing about a new, lower price, they often overpaid.

To solve this problem, we created a system to automate the communication. We included key people in the design process and worked hard to create the system. The system was finished on time and on budget. But the team members would not use the new system. Even though the system was easier to use than the previous tools, even though everyone agreed that we had a problem that needed to be solved and that the new system addressed that problem, and even though everyone agreed that this change was required to ensure the financial health of the organization, it was nearly impossible to get these very young people to use it. They did not want to change.

Young people are also creatures of habit, even when they understand that change is important. For the young people reading this book, observe how often you go to the same restaurants, drive on the same roads to get those restaurants, and often order the same menu items, time after time after time.

In order to get the team members to use the new system, we had to make it an imperative. In this case, unfortunately, we had report failures to use the new system to the bosses of the members of the team. Soon, everyone was using the new system. Soon, using the new system became the established habit.

While it is better to try to use positive reinforcements (there are binders of research that prove people respond better to rewards than punishments), every business transformation that I have led has required some method to make the transformation an imperative. This has been true with every transformation that I have been involved with, large and small. For the large business transformations that I have managed, people often have to feel like the very survival of the organization is at stake, or at least their survival in the organization.

Another way to understand our resistance to change is to consider the differences between our wants and our desires. As we will observe in a later chapter, much of our behavior is driven by our desires. But our "desires" are not the same as our "wants." For most of us, if we are asked to write down a list of the things that we want; we will make a very long list. Our list of wants is usually impossibly long. This is another characteristic of human nature. For most of us, we want many more things than we will ever have the resources to obtain.

This list goes beyond material things. Most of us want more friends than we have the time to cultivate. We want to visit more places than we will have the time to visit. We want more hours in the day, more dollars in the bank, more love in our relationships, more years in our life. In many ways, this is a positive human characteristic. Find the person with no more wants, and you will find the person with nothing left to live for.

Our desires, on the other hand, refer to the shorter list of things we will actually use our resources to get. These resources are not limited to finances, but include our emotional reserves and the hours of our day. In this sense, we are desire-driven life forms: Our desires focus our effort and our energy. Because of this human characteristic, a difficult transformation will not occur if we only "want" it to occur. Difficult transformations will not occur until they are compelling desires. What can we do to make an important transformation an imperative? What can we do to convert a "want" for a transformation into a compelling "desire" to change? We can learn one approach from Hernán Cortés, a Spanish conquistador.

In 1519, Captain Cortés embarked on one of the largest conquests in the history of the world, against the Aztec empire. Starting from the Spanish held island of Cuba, Cortés set sail with a small army for the beaches of Veracruz, where he and his men would experience their first victory. Three years later, Cortés and his army conquered the last Aztec stronghold. As a result of their victory, Spain ruled much of the land previously controlled by the Aztecs. To reward Cortés for this military achievement, the Spanish Crown made him the ruler over the area of current day Mexico. Cortés also built Mexico City into the most important European city in the Americas, and he ruled over 23,000 servants.

Cortés started the conquest with a very bold move. As a result of this decisive action, Cortés made sure that both he and his army were committed. He made success an imperative, a compelling desire that HAD to be achieved.

What was the bold move? When his army arrived at the shores of Veracruz, Cortés burned their boats. With the fiery embers of his ships sinking into the ocean, he cemented the imperative with this declaration to his army: "You can either fight, or you can die." Cortés permanently removed the option of retreat. By burning the boats, he transformed his ambition for conquest into victory for both him and the army.

Author and motivational speaker John Boe tells us how this same approach was used by the Greeks. "The ancient Greek warriors were both feared and respected by their enemies. In battle, the Greeks established a well-deserved reputation for their unsurpassed bravery and unshakable commitment to victory. The key to their overwhelming success on the battlefield had far more to do with how the Greek commanders motivated the warriors than it did with issues of tactics or training. The Greeks were master motivators who understood how to use a "dramatic demonstration" to infuse a spirit of commitment into the heart of every warrior. Once the warriors had been offloaded from their boats onto their enemy's shore, the Greek commanders would shout out their first order..."burn the boats!" The sight of burning boats removed any notion of retreat from their hearts and any thoughts of surrender from their heads. Imagine the tremendous psychological impact on the soldiers as they watched their boats being set to the torch. As the boats turned to ash and slipped quietly out of sight into the water, each man understood there was no turning back and the only way home was through victory."

Many great leaders have understood and used this principle to create imperatives among their people. George Patton used this principle as he led US troops in Europe during World War II. Walt Disney used this principle when leading his company to incredible achievements in the film industry. The great NFL Hall of Fame coach, Vince Lombardi, used this principle as he led the Greenbay Packers to multiple championships. These great leaders were successful creating imperatives, but can you learn this skill? The answer is an emphatic, YES!!!

My friend Melanie turned her transformation goal to lose weight into an imperative. She created the imperative by placing a bathroom scale next to her refrigerator and by writing her weight loss goals on a piece of paper, which she hung on the refrigerator door. Every time she would go to the refrigerator for a snack, she would get on the scale while she looked at her weight loss goals. Melanie lost over 40 pounds in six months by making her weight loss goal a compelling desire, by making her goal an imperative. Melanie had experienced several failed attempts to lose weight in the past, but the scale, and goals on her refrigerator, made this attempt a success.

My friend Jack turned his transformation goal to quit smoking cigarettes into an imperative by getting color photographs of tobacco destroyed lungs and hanging those pictures all over his house, in his car, and in his cubicle at work. He also hung pictures of people with rotten brown teeth that were destroyed by smoking tobacco in prominent places in his home. Jack also experienced several failed attempts to quit smoking, but the pictures of the damaging effects of tobacco were just what he needed to turn his "want" to quit smoking into a compelling desire – into an imperative.

I continue to achieve transformation goals in my personal life by listing them on a piece of paper that I hang on my bathroom mirror. I also track my success in achieving those goals by counting my daily successes and recording them on another piece of paper that I hang on that same mirror.

Communicating your transformation goals to people who you respect can also be a powerful tool. Most of us can be motivated to change through peer pressure, particularly positive peer pressure from people we respect.

In addition to sharing your transformation goals with people you respect, schedule recurring meetings with them so that you can report your successes to them. You will be surprised by the number of people who will be happy to help you in this way. Most people love helping other people change for the better, even if they are not good at it themselves.

All of these suggestions are examples of how you can figuratively "burn your boats" and make it harder for you to return to old habits. Whenever you embark on a journey of personal or organizational transformation, remember this important Second Principle:

Principle #2: Turn your transformation goal into an imperative – turn it into a compelling desire.

Burning Boats

CHAPTER THREE

TRAPPED BY A CURTAIN OF IDEAS

Gisela and I were watching the sun set over the Main River in Frankfurt Germany when we said our final goodbyes. The clear water of the Main River, so pristine, was a sharp reminder of the heavily polluted Elbe River that we had seen just a short time ago.

The two rivers provided a powerful metaphor symbolizing how my relationship with Gisela had changed. Like the Main River, today we could look at each other with clarity of understanding. We no longer felt like enemies. When we looked at the polluted Elbe River, a little more than one month before, we looked at each other through the polluted shadows of suspicion and distrust. Oh how much Gisela's life had changed in such a short period of time, as had mine!

When Gisela turned her head away from the Main River to look at me, I could see uncertainty and fear in her eyes. I could taste her fear; I could smell it. But her gaze was also full of anticipation, like the edgy look of a young woman in the last car of a rollercoaster. The cars in front of her have already disappeared over the crest into an uncertain future, but her car is slowing down to a deliberate and menacing stop in preparation for a dramatic plunge. She is clearly nervous, but appears hesitantly ready for the rapid and exhilarating descent ahead.

She appeared to be in a dilemma. Should she safely hold onto the handrails or throw her hands in the air in wild abandon? Is there even a handrail to hold onto? For a brief moment she appeared to be in ecstasy, feeling, suddenly, wide awake, as if the rest of her life had been spent in a fog. Her life had been spent in a fog, but an unforeseen hurricane had ripped that fog away.

I knew the look. I had experienced a massive mental whirlwind in my life when I was 17, which completely changed me for the better. I believed what Gisela was experiencing would similarly improve her life. But how could she know for sure? The previous five weeks had decimated much of what she thought was true. Her mind was gasping for air as it tried to comprehend the great deception that had surrounded her. She was experiencing a series of massive mental transformations. I, and the people who were traveling with me, had unwittingly played a small role in helping Gisela prepare for this transformation. I was grateful to see her once more to celebrate her new future.

*   *   *

Eight weeks earlier, when I was traveling to Czechoslovakia, I did not even know that Gisela was alive. Little would I have guessed that I was about to play a role in the destruction of her fabricated perception of the world.

The few days that I would spend in Czechoslovakia would partially prepare my mind for the moment when I would meet Gisela. Those days would build a narrow bridge of empathy in my mind, enabling the two of us to meet over a chasm of ideas that separated our polar-opposite views of the world.

It was late morning in October, 1989, when our bus approached the demilitarized zone that separated Austria from Communist Czechoslovakia. I was traveling with 35 other students, three professors and their spouses, and our bus driver Horst. As we approached the border of Czechoslovakia, we immediately felt the iron hand of Moscow – high fences, guard dogs, barbed wire, machine guns, hidden land mines, and corruption.

We had to wait for what seemed like an eternity at the crossing station. I watched through the front window of the bus as Dr. Tobler had a tense conversation with one of the Czech border guards. I could barely hear the mix of broken German and Czech phrases that passed between Dr. Tobler and the man with the machine gun. The guard was clearly trying to figure out how much we would pay; how "generous" could we afford to be? Dr. Tobler, tension plaguing his nervous face, continued to increase the amount. Before leaving Austria for Czechoslovakia we had been warned that some undefined "payment" would be required to enter Czechoslovakia. We had also been warned not to call the "payment" a bribe. Suddenly, I could see Dr. Tobler's face relax and I knew he and the armed guard had reached an acceptable agreement. He made the payment and we were allowed to proceed.

Driving into Communist Czechoslovakia was like entering a time machine. We were often surprised as we looked through our modern bus windows at horse drawn wagons and farmers working the soil by hand. There were no modern tractors, no gas-powered combines to be seen. The bricks on the buildings were brown, outdated, crumbling with age, and the old stone fences bordering the fields appeared as though they had become a seamless part of the landscape

By the time we reached Prague, the golden city of five hundred spires, it felt like we had traveled back 100 years. I looked down at my hands just to make sure I was still alive. Throughout Czechoslovakia, the electronic gadgets we had all become accustomed to, and many innovations from the previous 50 years, were nowhere to be found.

Several times I found myself intoxicated by the strange and magical atmosphere of the city. With cobblestone streets, small passageways, majestic castles, and morning fog, Prague emanated a special kind of beauty that lent itself to dark nights and evening enchantment.

Even before the First and Second World Wars, Prague was called the Paris of the East because of its breathtaking gothic buildings. Over a thousand years of astounding architecture has created a three-dimensional visual masterpiece. The magic of Prague has been maintained because it is the only great European city from the Middle Ages that was not bombed during World War II. In a state of visual drunkenness, I was almost deceived by the government's attempt to use this majestic city as a blinder against a true evil. However, their attempt to create a façade of good wealth and prosperity was not so easily swallowed.

The inexpensive and diverse assortment of food contributed to the charade, as did the value of the American dollars in my pocket. With a small wad of $5 bills, I felt like an aristocrat in the middle ages. My friends and I were quickly addicted to the incredible 25 cent pastries and the seven-course gourmet dinners that we could savor for under $10. We also enjoyed Reduta, Prague's oldest and best-known jazz club. In fewer than five years Bill Clinton would be there, playing his saxophone to a boisterous crowd.

Descending the stairs to the cellar where Reduta was located was like entering a reverse time machine. We left the dated streets of Prague above us and entered a world of music that made us feel like we were back in America. Music has the power to bridge even the most dramatic ideological chasms. However, even in the jazz club, we would be jolted back behind the Iron Curtain when the Czech musicians would attempt to sing in English. The results were broken words, just like the broken society. Incredible food, music, world-renowned architecture – it was all being used in an attempt to deceive us.

As they had intended, the mind-bending magic emanated by the beauty of Prague was enchanting enough to fool me – for a moment. It almost made me forget about the structured brutality that existed around every street corner of a city that was completely controlled by what had become a cruel Communist regime.

But I was not fooled and I did not forget where I was. The director of our study abroad program, Doug Tobler, made sure that we stopped in the city of Tabor on our way to Prague. Tabor was a Czechoslovakian town located half way between Prague and the Austrian border. We stopped there because Dr. Tobler wanted us to see how most Czechoslovakians lived. The deprivation we saw in Tabor was heart wrenching. Like the cities we had already toured in Communist Hungary and Yugoslavia, the poverty was impossible to hide. It was like walking into a black and white movie of Oliver Twist. There was almost no food in the major Tabor grocery store, and the food that was available had no appeal, partly because there was no color in anything. There was no color in their food, in their clothes, in their "modern" construction. How can whole nations of people live without color? I guess the central economic planners of the Communist economic machine decided that color was just something that people could live without.

All the magnificent buildings had clearly been built during another age; an age that preceded the debilitating ideologies that had brought Czechoslovakia (one of the most advanced democracies before World War II) under the iron claws of Communism. During our trip, we learned first hand that Prague was one of the few "model" cities where the communist machine tried to deceptively show off its economic achievements to western diplomats. The pastries, the fancy meals, and even the jazz club, were part of a planned scheme to hide the general failure of communism and its inability to meet the basic needs of its citizens.

I was not fooled because I had spent some time studying free-market economics (capitalism) and planned economics (socialism and communism). The Soviet Union, which controlled Czechoslovakia, had attempted to use an extreme form of communism. Virtually nothing could be traded legally without the interference of central planning committees, who did things such as set the prices on all merchandise, services, and wages. In the simplest form, that meant that if a farmer walking down the street with a bushel of carrots passed a farmer with a bag of potatoes, they could not legally trade so many carrots for so many potatoes. To prevent this kind of "illegal" activity, much of the farming and production was taken over by the government. The extreme central planning used by the Soviet Union also forbade anyone from making money from any of their inventions.

The net effect of this intervention was economic failure. People lacked motivation to work hard and they lacked incentive to invent anything to improve their lives or to improve the processes or tools of production.

One thing that was produced in relative abundance was Vodka. With few other ambitions to pursue in their constrained lives, many people living under the controls of the Soviet Union simply drowned their minds in alcohol.

A broken economic machine drowned in alcohol is not what the founders of the Soviet experiment intended. The original ideas that brought almost 60% of the world's population under some form of socialist rule sought to achieve greater economic equality among working people. The founders of the Soviet Union taught that the principles of capitalism were a web of lies that would be used by the rich to gain an increasing percentage of the world's wealth.

Under the communist plan, the wealth would be shared more equally and everyone would have a job. It was an intoxicating idea and was initially implemented by ideological leaders with a compelling vision and charisma. However, a fundamental principle of human nature proved to be too difficult to overcome: It is nearly impossible for most people to work hard unless they benefit from their work. It was because of this human characteristic that so many people stopped working altogether.

By the time it became clear that communism would not be economically viable, the Soviet political machine had already been created. Like virtually all political machines, this monster took on a life of its own and began to protect itself from extinction. The failed experiment of communism also motivated the smartest and most ambitious Soviet citizens to flee to the west to seek their own fortune and gain control over their lives. This flight of talent led to the introduction of a new phrase: Brain Drain.

In just one day, August 12th, 1961, a record 4,000 people crossed the border from East Berlin to West Berlin to start a new life. The Soviet political machine decided that a Brain Drain was probably not good for its survival so it began to build walls to keep the ambitious and disloyal unbelievers from leaving. In the early hours of August 13th, 1961, "shock workers" from East Germany and Russia shut off the border between the Soviet and western sectors of Berlin using barbed wire. The Soviet power continued to build fences and walls around all of its borders. Over time, those barriers would stretch over 2,000 miles along the western border of the Soviet Union alone.

But walls were not designed to hold in an entire population. Walls can constrain small numbers of criminals, like they do in penal institutions. Electrified fences and barbed wire can hold prisoners of war in POW camps. But bricks and mortar, even with barbed wire and electricity, cannot hold in a nation. The challenge: A government cannot hire the prisoners inside a wall to guard themselves. A citizen will reliably break down over time and allow his countrymen to pass through. Why shouldn't he? Those men are his allies. They should be allowed to do as they please.

To hold in a nation you need something much stronger than walls; something even much stronger than barbed wire, land mines, and machine guns. To hold a nation in, you need the most powerful human constraint ever discovered. You have to use the power of ideas.

In an effort to combat the declining enthusiasm for the principles of communism, the Soviet propaganda machine kicked into high gear. The fundamental ideas that were initially taught were fairly simple. They started with popular ideas like, "The good of the many outweigh the good of the few" or, "People seeking their own interest are selfish and evil." The propaganda machine also continued to attack the ideas that supported Western Capitalism.

The attack on western ideas became more difficult as the West began to transmit radio and television signals across the Soviet border. Those transmissions contained a painful message for the Soviet citizens: Westerners appeared to enjoy significantly more wealth than the Soviets could imagine and they enjoyed many new inventions.

Put yourself in their shoes. Imagine what it would be like if you could only see others enjoy new inventions like cassette tapes and then CDs, cell phones, laser printers, walkmans, roller blades, ATMs, the nonstick Teflon pan, birth control pills. The list of new inventions in the West went on and on. The poor Soviets could only watch these fascinating new things through television images.

To circumvent this counter attack, the Soviet Union enforced laws that forbade their citizens from watching western television or listening to western radio. They also stated that the television images, coming from the west, which displayed seemingly unbounded wealth, only represented the richest of the western people. The propaganda portrayed those rich people as greedy exploiters, who only enjoyed their wealth because the western workers lived in abject poverty. Through propaganda, the Soviet Union built a curtain of ideas to blind its people from recognizing its own economic failures. That curtain of ideas was so strong it would eventually be called the Iron Curtain. This Iron Curtain of ideas completely surrounded Gisela's mind when we first met her in the tragic city of Dresden.

*   *   *

It was unfortunate that we had to meet Gisela for the first time in Dresden. Because of the pain that had been visited upon that city, her mind was understandably wrapped in the ideologies of the Iron Curtain. To the East Germans, Dresden was a well-known symbol of western brutality. Dresden had the grandeur of Paris and Prague before World War II and the western nations destroyed it. It was as simple as distorting several facts and, bingo: The Communist government had a concrete example of the unthinkable cruelties of the capitalist West.

The Allied Powers (the U.S., England, etc.) tried an experiment on Dresden that had failed many times before in world history. The Allied Powers knew that the German people were very proud of Dresden, because of its history and architecture. As a way of delivering a hard punch to the citizens of Germany, the Allies completely obliterated the city with bombs.

Between February 13th and February 14th 1945, 1,300 planes dropped 3,900 tons of bombs on 13 square miles, killing around 30,000 people. The Allied Powers did this with the hope that the utter destruction of a beautiful landmark would weaken the will of the German people and cause them to surrender. The experiment failed. It invigorated the will of the German people to fight and probably extended the carnage of World War II for several months. For the people living in East Germany, this attack still served as a reminder of how cruel the Western people were. Just being in Dresden probably increased Gisela's initial disdain for the bus-load of American "exploiters" that she was preparing to meet.

Gisela was a government appointed tour guide of the Deutsche Demokratische Republik (DDR), which was the official name for East

Germany. All tour groups that wanted to visit the DDR had to be accompanied by an official tour guide at all times. This was particularly enforced with Western tour groups like ours.

For the next week, Gisela would not leave our side for even an hour as we explored the depressing attractions of the DDR. At 23 years old, our tour guide was a mere two years younger than I was. Like me, Gisela was a university student. She was preparing herself in the hopes of becoming a valuable member of her society. She was a promising young member of the Communist Party, having studied at a university in Moscow.

Gisela was an idealist. I could see it in the way she spoke to us, the way she related the facts, the way she seemingly snubbed her nose at the rest of the world. Like me, she had clearly spent inordinate amounts of time thinking about her own ideas. Probably because of the time she had spent in introspection, Gisela had a bounce in her step that reflected confidence. Her perspective was correct. Ours was not. It was as simple as that.

Unfortunately, Gisela was a devout Communist. Her perspective was therefore restricted, shadowed, and had been tampered with by the controlled atmosphere of the Soviet propaganda machine. In this respect, Gisela was separated from most of the students that were in our group by a large ideological chasm. Another factor made the chasm even wider: All of Gisela's previous tour groups were from the Soviet Union. We were the first "westerners" that she had ever met.

The Communist Regime had explained to Gisela that the only kind of people from the west that could afford to tour the DDR for five days were from the class of the "rich exploiters." I wanted so badly to tell her how poor I had been, how I had lived on the streets for years, how I was very much removed from the upper classes of society. It was impossible, however, to say anything. The ideological chasm was too deeply carved in her mind. She would have heard nothing of the sort. She KNEW what she had been told. She would not listen to a conniving westerner. Not a chance. For Gisela, we were the embodiment of evil. We were the exploiters that the Iron Curtain was designed to protect her from.

I watched Gisela closely over the next several days. I wanted to see how she would react as she got to know us. How would she change as she found out that we were not the evil creatures that she had been warned about? My understanding of how our ideas shape who we are told me that I was about to see a human transformation. I was right. Her changes were like watching the metamorphosis of a caterpillar into a butterfly. Her initial reactions had clearly shown her disdain for what she thought we represented: The Exploiters.

As we traveled together, the ideas planted in her head began to clash with her direct perceptions of who we really were. These conflicting viewpoints were obvious during several embarrassing moments for her, and for us, as our different expectations of the world collided. Gisela was the victim of the first embarrassing moment, which occurred on our first day together. We were walking across the bridge that spans the Elbe River in Meissen, on our way to the Albrechtsburg Castle. I paused on the bridge to view the river. I was sickened by the image that assaulted my eyes. The water in the Elbe was grotesquely polluted. It was milky brown, and some sort of purple liquid would occasionally bubble to the surface. It was the most polluted river I had ever seen.

As I turned my head to continue across the bridge, I locked eyes with Gisela. She had been watching me. She abruptly looked down, apparently in shame. In that brief moment she could see that I was revolted by the polluted river and she knew that I was not used to seeing this. Something told her that the pollution surrounding her was inconsistent with a 50-year plan to bring wealth and prosperity to the masses.

I'll bet Gisela wondered what the rivers in America looked like. She had probably assumed the worst. But seeing the reaction on my face, she began to wonder: What if the rivers in America are clean? How do these Exploiters keep their rivers clean? What if these Exploiters are not really the bad guys after all? What if they are just regular people, not exploiting anyone?

*   *   *

In our youth hotel in Leipzig, something would happen to embarrass us all.

The hotel was surprisingly posh. The communist government built extravagant youth hotels in an attempt to counter the other economic failures that surrounded the lives of the children of their failing system.

After checking into our rooms we gathered in the dining room to eat. Food had already been prepared and was laid out on a table for us. We were pleasantly surprised. There were a couple choices of sliced meat and a couple types of cheese. The food was better than anything we had eaten since Prague. It was clearly better than the stale bread we had for lunch in Meissen. We had to settle for the bread because the only other food that particular restaurant offered was tripe soup. I had heard of tripe, which is made from cow stomach, but I had never actually seen it. We were pleased by the spread at the youth hotel.

Looking back on that experience, I think we could have shown better etiquette. But we were hungry, so we quickly ate the food on the table. Darcy, one of the girls from our group turned to Gisela and asked "When is the main dish coming?"

Gisela was unable to hold her composure. A frown of disbelief formed on her face when she replied "That was everything that we have."

We all thought the meats and cheeses were the appetizer. We might have eaten a little slower, savored the food, if we had known this was all we were getting.

Another girl from our group, still hungry, pleaded "Surely there is more?"

Gisela, now embarrassed, as she stood alone, in front of all of us, stuttered slightly "There is no more; you have eaten the best food we have to offer."

A hush descended upon our group as we came to terms with our insensitivity, born out of an acquaintance with plenty.

So the hours proceeded… We would be shocked by the absence of things like decent food or any food, color postcards or any postcards, or even toilet paper. And, in turn, Gisela would be shocked by our high expectations. But none of these incidences would prepare us for the events at the Berlin Wall. To help emphasize the contrast of poverty and wealth between East and West Germany, Dr. Tobler planned to have us visit West Berlin for a couple of hours. It was made clear that we would only be allowed on the other side of the Berlin wall for a couple of hours and then we would have to come back to the poverty of the Soviet empire.

We were excited as the bus crawled through the slow line toward the border crossing. The Wall stood high in front of us, and we watched expectantly as it drew nearer. We had never seen anything quite like this. In America, the only walls one could not cross were in the prisons or the government district. It was a foreign idea to us that there could be a boundary placed in the center of a city.

We could not wait to cross. Perhaps we would eat a Big Mac or maybe some ice cream. It may be hard to believe that we were craving Big Macs, but we had been in Czechoslovakia and East Germany for over a week and were tired of things like tripe soup. Our anticipation mounted as we approached the gate where the East Berlin border guards performed their duties. Our enthusiasm was shattered at the guard gate. We were shocked when we heard the forceful proclamation of the border guard: Gisela could not continue with us.

While our interactions over the last couple of days had strained both parties, we were growing fond of our DDR tour guide. How could it be possible that she could not cross the border? Even for only a couple of hours!

The border guard was very clear. Gisela could not go. In fact, this was probably as close as she had ever gotten to the world outside of the Iron Curtain. With only two or three steps she could actually reach that other world, but the price for taking those two or three steps would be her life. The guard would shoot her dead. No questions.

I could see Gisela's mind churning as she faced the brutality and painful resolve of the guard's words. His leather gloves gripped a handheld machine gun, and his eyes focused down on us like cold steel. A blackbird flew across the sky, across the wall. The bird looked down on us and continued to float away. Gisela watched him, a prisoner of her own weight and political convictions.

Gisela had to ask herself: Why couldn't she be allowed to enter the west for only a couple of hours? What was she not supposed to see? What was she not supposed to hear? In our resulting grief from knowing we would lose our guide at the border, we asked Gisela if there was anything we could buy for her in West Berlin. We made it abundantly clear that the sky was the limit. Anything she wanted, we would buy. ANYTHING. But, our generosity was not something that Gisela could relate to. She did not live in a world where people could afford to be generous. Her response shocked us. She wanted only two things: hair barrettes (the cloth covered rubber bands that are used to make pony tails) and grapes. She had not had grapes in 8 years. How strange this was to us.

That moment completely changed Gisela's perspective. It was her supposedly beneficent government that would not let her cross the border, while we, the so-called exploiters, were the ones that would give her anything she wanted. How could she reconcile everything that she had been taught with this experience? Because Gisela could not go with us, she got out of the bus and waited for our return. I am sure that these were some of the longest hours of her life.

*   *   *

After returning to East Berlin, we spent a couple more days with Gisela, as we drove to the border that separated the entire countries of East and West Germany. Our interactions with Gisela over those couple of days were quite somber. She was clearly distraught. The cherished ideas in her mind were beginning to collapse. These were the ideas that she had used to build her mental picture of the world, and they were corroding and breaking away from one another. She didn't know what to think, much less what to make of our presence and impact.

We did not know what to say or what to do because we knew that soon we would have to leave her at another border, and this time we would leave her for the rest of her life. We no longer complained about anything. The depravations that we experienced in her country of lies bombarded us and we took them with our heads down. We no longer attempted to defend our political or economic ideals. We knew that any statement we made in this area would be like throwing salt on a fresh but festering and painful wound. She no longer reacted defensively when she saw our frustrations, now unspoken, from the lack of services that we took for granted in the west, like toilet paper.

Gisela had figured out that we were not the embodiment of evil. She now knew that we were just regular people trying to find a little happiness during life's journey.

The mental pain that Gisela was experiencing was intensified as we stopped in the towns of Wittenberg and Eisenach. These towns had great historic significance, but Gisela seemed less interested in her duties as tour guide and more interested in figuring out the extent of the lies her government had told her.

Wittenberg was the town where Martin Luther is said to have defiantly posted a paper with 95 ideas on the door of the Castle Church in 1517. These 95 ideas challenged the teachings of the Roman Catholic Church on the nature of penance, the authority of the pope, and the usefulness of indulgences. In Martin Luther's day, indulgences were sometimes represented by a piece of paper that a person could purchase from a priest for the remission of their sins. In effect, indulgences made people think that they could buy forgiveness from God with money. Martin Luther did not agree with the idea that we could pay a priest to have our sins forgiven.

Eisenach is the town where the Wartburg Castle is located. It was in the Wartburg castle that Martin Luther hid, in the year 1521, while he translated the New Testament into German. He believed that if the New Testament was the word of God, then everyone should be able to read it. It was a revolutionary concept for the time. In fact, posting the 95 ideas on the Castle Church door in Wittenberg and translating the

Bible were actions that created world-altering mental tremors for many generations to come. These actions created ideas that have since changed the lives of millions and millions of people, both inside and outside the Roman Catholic Church. In part, Martin Luther's ideas gave birth to the Protestant Reformation, which helped give birth to the Enlightenment, and later to the concepts of democracy and freedom that we enjoy today.

It was painful to realize that Gisela was imprisoned mentally and physically by a relatively new set of ideas. These new ideas actually prevented her from continuing on a highway heading southwest with her new friends. As soon as those new friends crossed a physical line on the ground she would have to stop. This line was called the Iron Curtain. The cycle of the ages had repeated itself. Someone needed to free this girl from captivity. As we rode along our thoughts drifted toward freeing Gisela, but there was nothing we could do. There was nothing anyone could do except those in charge. Or was there? Maybe the power rested within each of us, just like it had within Martin Luther, 450 years ago.

When we left Gisela to return to West Germany, I felt like I was abandoning a baby girl who had just opened her eyes. It was a somber departure for all of us. We would return to countries with relatively unlimited opportunities and she would remain a prisoner – perhaps never seeing another grape.

Little did we know that the Iron Curtain would completely collapse in only a few short weeks. We would see Gisela again, and this time we would see her in our ideological world.

*   *   *

We were pleased when we heard that Gisela would meet us in Frankfurt in her first trip outside of the fallen Iron Curtain. Soon after Giesela entered West Germany, she was astounded when she saw that the poorest people who lived there were richer than almost anyone who had been living behind the Iron Curtain. Her first visit to a western grocery store was the most shocking experience of all. She fell to her in knees, in front of everyone, and wept uncontrollably. She was amazed by the variety and unlimited quantity of things she could buy, including unlimited hair barrettes of multiple colors. She was shocked by the variety and quality of the grapes.

My reunion with Gisela at the Main River in Frankfurt was tender. My six-month journey in Europe had come to an end. It was a journey that would alter the rest of my life in very positive ways. I am happy to say, it was a journey that also helped change the life of Gisela.

Watching Gisela change reminded me of the mental transformations that occurred in my mind when I was 17. Somehow, a boy who was thought to be beyond all hope had turned away from severe chemical addictions, repeated crime, multiple arrests, budding connections to organized crime, and a very likely early death.

I turned away from that path through the power of ideas. New ideas had directed me to a new path of abundance and happiness. In my case, the change was caused by a spiritual awakening. Through multiple experiences, I came to the conclusion that God is real. As I began to adopt a spiritual belief system in my life, I replaced old, debilitating ideas with new, enriching ones. As I adopted those new ideas, I completely changed. In less than one year, I transformed from a gun-toting, drug-dealing criminal, to a Bible-reading, sober Christian. The change was so transforming that I decided to serve a Mormon mission, and spent two years working and saving nearly every penny so that I could spend another 18 months serving that mission.

The change was very unexpected and dramatic. However, the transformation that I experienced was not unique. Many people have completely changed their lives through a conversion to religions of multiple kinds, both Christian and non-Christian alike. Other people have also changed their lives in major ways as they have adopted significant non-religious belief systems that were new to them, like communism, utilitarianism, capitalism, environmentalism, vegetarianism... Giesla experienced dramatic changes as her ideas about communism and free market economies changed. I experienced dramatic changes when my ideas about God, religion, and the purpose of my life changed.

*   *   *

How and why do ideas have such an impact on human behavior?

One way to answer this question is to look at forms of life that are not influenced by ideas at all. It is not hard to find these other life forms. You can't miss them. There are literally hundreds of thousands of species whose behavior is not driven, or even influenced, by ideas. Some of these other life forms are completely driven by the dictatorial chemical blueprints that come from instincts. As I define the term, an instinct is an automatic form of knowledge. An instinct is knowledge that a life form possesses from the beginning of its existence – knowledge that does not have to be learned.

Virtually all plants and insects are completely driven by the inherited, genetic, chemical rules of instincts. Not only are these life forms not influenced by ideas, they do not even have the capacity to perceive an idea. Like a computer that can only do what it is told through software programs, these organisms survive through hard-wired chemical programs.

As a result of this hard-wiring, these life forms have one distinct advantage: They require no training from their parents. A tree seed requires no training from its parent tree. An amoeba requires no training from its parent amoeba. At the beginning of their existence, these lower life forms are immediately independent. They do not have to learn anything to survive!

This is clearly not true of humans. If we are lucky, we may only require 20 years of training before we can become independent and flourish – 20 years!!! For various reasons, some of us, with apparently healthy brains and bodies, never seem to achieve meaningful independence at all. In fact, if our nurturing is highly deficient, we may not even survive.

It is true that some of our actions are driven by instincts, like the requirement that we sleep and the requirement that our bodies digest food, but these biological functions do not have to be learned and they represent a very small portion of human behavior. Most of our behaviors are learned. So, while the lowest-level life forms, like plants and insects, are completely driven by instincts, human beings are primarily driven by what we learn: by our ideas!

We are idea-driven life forms.

Compared to humans, life forms that are driven solely by instincts have a major disadvantage. These lower life forms have a very low capacity to adapt to new environments or to changes in their environment. In order to survive, lower-level life forms have to be brought into the world in environments that are highly aligned with their instincts. For example, very few insects or plants that flourish at the equator could survive in Alaska. Very few insects or plants that flourish in a desert could even survive in a rain forest. These life forms are independent from their parent life form from the beginning of their existence, but they have a very limited ability to adapt to changes in their environment.

We, on the other hand, can have amazing adaptation skills. Human beings live in virtually every kind of physical environment on the face of the earth. Some live in submarines, some in outer space, and some even spend much of their time living in the man-made virtual worlds created by innovative computer software engineers. I am convinced that we will eventually inhabit other planets, like the moon, or maybe even other dimensions that we cannot yet perceive. Human beings have an amazing capacity to adapt! In fact, when compared to other forms of life, our ability to change and adapt may be our most differentiating and important characteristic.

However, like virtually all human skills, adaptation skills, or transformation skills, have to be learned. We are born with a virtually unlimited capacity to adapt. But we are not born with the skills to adapt – we have to learn those skills! We cannot become effective at adapting or at transforming our lives until we learn the principles that govern human transformation. To truly learn those principles, we have to perceive, comprehend, accept, and practice them. But, before we can even perceive or comprehend those skills, we have to believe that we can change and we have to want to change. This may be one of the greatest paradoxes associated with human nature: we have an almost unlimited capacity to change, but we cannot take advantage of that capacity until we choose to.

These truths were reinforced when I saw a monumental change occur in Gisela's ideas and life in Germany and in my own ideas and life at 17. If my life is a testimony to any principle, it is a testimony to the true principle that people can change, and they can change in very profound ways, and those changes are almost always caused by a change in their ideas. I have completely changed from the person who burglarized Erma J. Staffen's home on Thanksgiving Day in 1976, and I continue to experience profound changes in my life and in my perspective of the universe.

In all of the business turnarounds that I have managed, changing people's ideas has been a critical part of the turnaround. In every case, at the beginning of the turnaround, many team members did not think that the transformation objective would be successful. In every case, one of the most important actions we had to take was to help the team members begin to see that success was possible. In every case, full success was not attainable until most of the team members believed that it would occur. In every case, we had to start by changing the ideas in people's minds before other meaningful changes could even start.

The same mental changes are even more important in personal turnarounds. Personal turnarounds rarely occur until the person affected believes that the transformation can be successful.

Through my personal experience, through Gisela's experience, and through many other transformations that I have seen, led, or studied, I have learned this very important principle: As human beings, we are substantially controlled by the ideas we accept. I have also learned a most cherished truth: By changing what we believe, we can change who we are.

For human beings, ideas are very powerful things. In the words of Victor Hugo, "More powerful than an invading army is an idea whose time has come." In the words of Frank Lloyd Wright, "An idea is salvation by imagination." At least good ideas can bring salvation through imagination. Whenever you embark on a journey of personal or organizational transformation remember this important Third Principle:

Principle #3: By changing what you believe, you change who you are.

Trapped By A Curtain of Ideas

CHAPTER FOUR

MIND TO MUSCLE TO METAMORPHOSIS

Robert Hartness died in the spring of 2003. I was sad that I missed his funeral. Robert was a loyal companion during one of the most dangerous periods of my youth. We ended up taking different paths with our lives. His death did not come as a total surprise to me. Our different paths took us to different places, and the lifestyle he maintained was destined for catastrophe.

When I heard about Robert's death, I was 2,000 miles away from the city where he was buried. Before he died, it felt like we were separated, mentally and physically, by 2,000 light years. Despite our separation, my memory of the night Robert demonstrated his friendship and loyalty to me is still very vivid in my mind. That night was the first time I was robbed.

*   *   *

It was the fall of 1979 and I was living in Apple Valley, a very dark neighborhood on the outskirts of Augusta, Georgia. Apple Valley was darker than other places in the town. It was the violence that made it that way. There were gang fights in Apple Valley at a time when gang fights were unheard of outside of very large cities. I remember one gang fight which landed a friend of mine in the hospital because he was hit in the head with a steel pipe – blood, stitches, bandages. That fight started because kids from a nearby neighborhood drove by and gave someone a dirty look. We fought over really important stuff in Apple Valley.

I shared a house with Cheryl, who was a strip dancer at a club called Lucifer's Follies, which was located next to a club called The Whipping Post. I lost track of Cheryl many years ago. I'm sad when I think about her today, when I reflect on the high probability that she is probably not in a good place, if she is even alive.

Cheryl's story was like that of many of my friends at that time: sexually abused at a young age, emotionally abandoned, strung out on drugs, lost. On the few occasions when my mind was not completely altered with drugs, I worried about her three children who lived in the hell hole we called a house. We often woke them with our late-night drug parties. Sometimes fights would break out in the house, right in front of them. The home was like hell on earth, especially for kids. I sometimes entertained the fantasy of kidnapping the kids and taking them to a better place – as if I knew of any better place...

I was only 16, but I was already a big-shot drug dealer. I drove a powerful Pontiac Grand Prix and carried guns. Unlike Ellery, who was the other big drug dealer in the neighborhood, I was merely dealing drugs for fun. Ellery was serious about the drug business, and had a good system worked out.

You had to call Ellery in advance and meet him in the woods behind his house. And, you'd better come alone. Shortly after I moved into the neighborhood, Ellery was robbed and put out of business for several weeks. But Ellery was a street savvy business person, so he sent his customers to me. His rationale: if he was able to help his customers get what they were looking for, maybe they would come back

123

to him the next time they were feeding their addiction.

I was younger than Ellery, and therefore less sophisticated. It was much easier to do business with me. All you had to do was stop by my house and ring the door bell – ding dong. Because I was easier to do business with, I kept many of Ellery's customers after he was back in business. One day Ellery called in an attempt to resolve this competitive problem. I answered the phone.

"Hey Skip?" (Ellery called me Skip)

"Ellery, what's up?"

"Apple Valley's not big enough for the two of us."

I couldn't help but laugh in response to his statement. It sounded like a stupid line from an old cowboy movie.

He responded "This isn't anything to laugh about, you little punk."

"Where you moving to?" I said.

He responded again "You won't be laughing when I break your arms, white boy."

I had had enough of this conversation. "Listen Ellery, my Dad's in the Syndicate, and we have friends in Waynesboro who will bury black people for free."

Ellery hung up without a word.

Ellery knew the Syndicate was a powerful, mainly white drug gang.

My statements to Ellery on the phone were not true. At least I was not connected to organized crime through my father and I did not know anyone in Waynesboro that would bury people for free. But, I was a drug dealer. If I wasn't tough, if I wasn't a totally insensitive animal, I wouldn't stand a chance.

As I look back on the memory, I am amazed this interaction with Ellery did not end in violence, particularly because Ellery beat up everyone else who tried to sell drugs in Apple Valley. But that wasn't the first or last time Ellery and I would have problems with one another. Ellery and I had several other dangerous encounters. The first occurred shortly after I moved to Apple Valley.

Within a week of moving into the neighborhood, I sold magic mushrooms to a friend of his – earthy, spongy, psychedelic shrooms. Unfortunately, a poisonous mushroom was somehow mixed in with the psychedelic ones. Ellery and his friend boiled the poisonous mushroom with the psychedelic ones and ended up in the hospital. The poisonous mushroom almost killed them.

Ellery and I would knock heads again when one of the neighborhood punks stole Ellery's gun and sold it to me. Ellery called again.

"Hey Skip?"

"Made any recent trips to Waynesboro?" I asked.

Ellery ignored my smart-ass question and stated "You got my gun."

"Describe it" I said.

He described it.

"Yep, I got your gun."

"I want it, now!"

"Little Jimmy sold it to me for twenty-five bucks. For twenty-five, you can have it back."

"You won't be leaving your house tomorrow" he threatened.

"Ellery, I got your gun," I responded. This time, I hung up on him, the arrogant jerk.

Even though Ellery had a long history of violence and was large and strong (he spent all of his time doing drugs and lifting weights), he never attacked me. Perhaps he recognized my psychological wounds. Maybe, from his own experience, he could tell the initial emotional cuts occurred when I was very young. By now, the wounds were deep. Maybe he could see the truth behind my cold eyes. I was only 16, but I had an unlimited supply of drugs, I carried and owned several guns, and I lived with a strip dancer. He recognized I was not someone to screw with. He was right.

*   *   *

Despite my tough-guy attitude, I was not in the drug business to build a fortune. What would I do with a fortune? I frequently wondered if I would even be alive the very next day. So I spent every penny I made on drug parties at my house. I was not judgmental; anyone could come to my parties, even if they were only 13 years old. After all, I was also pulled into the world of dope at a very young age.

Depending on the night and the availability, I served up a smorgasbord of addiction. I always had pot and alcohol, but I often had mushrooms or LSD. I reserved my cocaine supply for close friends. Because of my generosity, I started to attract people to my home that had even darker minds than mine, people like Jake.

Jake was several years older than me, maybe twenty. Our appearance was similar: both about six feet tall, long dishwater blond hair, and skinny, drug-emaciated bodies. Like me, Jake always carried a weapon, but his preference was a knife. But, Jake had a darker anger in his eyes. A couple years later I would hear about Jake getting into a fight with a pretty girl from our neighborhood. Jake banged her head on a cement sidewalk several times.

Something was wrong with Jake's mind. The anger he carried was deeper, stronger, and harsher than I had typically experienced or seen, even with the tough crowds I ran with. There are people in this world who behave like rabid animals. Jake was one of them. He often sold me harder drugs, like Meth, which was hard to find at that time in Georgia, and Methylenedioxyamphetamine, or MDA for short. I also paid Jake a premium to show me the field where I could pick magic mushrooms. Jake sold mushrooms from that field to anyone who would pay for them, but I paid him more to show me the field so that I could pick shrooms whenever I wanted to. You did not have to talk to Jake for long to guess his history. He was the victim of child abuse, violence, early drug use, violence, crime, more violence. It was painful to even look at him.

*   *   *

It was a Friday night and the lives of Robert Hartness, Jake, and I threatened to converge in a tragic way. Business had been good tonight. It was only 7 p.m. and my marijuana supply was sold out. This was great for cash flow, but the phone was still ringing off the hook – ring, ring, ring. People were anxiously looking to satisfy their addictions. I was the candy man, and I didn't have anymore candy. It wasn't always about the money in the drug dealing business. You had to keep your customers. You were no good to anybody if you were sold out.

Randy, my usual supplier, was at a party in the countryside beyond Waynesboro. It was borderline impossible to contact him. How could I replenish my supply to meet my customer's needs? Shortly after I ran out, Jake called me to see if I needed any more MDA.

"Hey man," I said. "I'm out of weed. I need to pick up something."

"How much you want?"

"Anything over a quarter pound. Anything less would be a waste of time."

"Alright," Jake said. He sounded drunk or high. Probably both. He fiddled around with something and kept me on the line. I heard music in the background and the voice of a girl. Or maybe it was two people arguing. I could hear Jake flipping through some papers. You'd think I was talking to a car dealership the way he handled it. "I got a buddy of mine who's got pounds going for..." he told me a good price. A really good price.

"I'll take one."

"Alright, meet me at Don's place down by the grocery store. I'll be there in twenty minutes. We'll ride up to my buddy's house together. He likes it when I take MY car, that way he knows nobody's screwing him."

"I'll be there in twenty minutes."

After I picked Jake up, we took the Grand Prix, my car, to go pick up the weed. Jake's car was missing. He claimed he had no idea where it was. This was the type of stuff that happened in our lives almost every day. Not knowing where your car was, or who was driving it, was as common as eating eggs for breakfast.

"Alright, turn in right here," said Jake. "Where's the dough?"

I patted a lump in my front pocket.

"Give it to me."

"What? No."

"Come ON, he's not going to let you come in. He doesn't know you. This guy's really crazy, man… crazier than ME."

I swallowed. Jake was really crazy. I handed him the cash.

"Alright, he takes forever sometimes, so just wait out here till I come back."

"Like how long?"

"I don't know, this guy's crazy, man… he likes to talk a lot."

"Tell him to hurry up!"

"I'll try, I'll try…"

My adrenaline was pulsing as Jake stepped out of the car and walked casually toward the building. He moved so confidently even though he was brittle and strung-out. He was on his last legs, desperate. Anyone could see it.

I sat out there for too long, almost 30 minutes, then went up and banged on the door with one hand on my gun under my coat.

"Who the hell is it?" A gruff voice shouted.

"It's Acid Face," I made up a moniker to avoid being remembered.

"I don't know no Acid Face?" the man asked. I nearly busted out laughing at the absurdity of the name.

"Where's Jake?"

"Who the hell is Jake?"

"He came in here about 30 minutes ago. He's supposed to be... you know..."

"No, I DON'T know," the voice yelled. "A guy named JIM got out of your car, came to the door asking if we had extra dog food, and went out the back door."

"What the..." These people were insane. Either Jake was hiding inside, or maybe he'd really flown the coop.

"Get out of here before I blow you down the steps."

I backed away, cursing. I could almost feel the bullets slapping my back. They never came.

On the drive back to my home in Apple Valley, I knew I could not let this insult go

131

unpunished. Even in those relatively harmless days, drug dealers stayed alive because they punished the people who crossed them. Tonight was one of those nights when I would have to again demonstrate my nasty side.

Even though I had grown accustomed to violence, I decided to get drugged up on a cocktail of meth and MDA before I left the house to hunt Jake down. Setting my gun on the table, I waited in Apple Valley for an hour to let the drug cocktail take its full effect. Ironically, Jake was the person that sold me the meth and MDA a couple days before.

By the time the hour was up, all of the usual groupies who hung around my house for the free drugs were gone. I guess the sight of my gun on the table and my talk of revenge scared them away. Most of them were pretty young anyway. Everyone was gone, that is, except for Robert Hartness. Robert was a loyal friend, and there was no way he was going to let me go alone.

Robert was partially raised by a mean but wise older brother. He never really spoke about his father. Some people, I assumed, simply didn't have fathers. It was a fact of life in my world. When Robert was still in grade school he came home one day and told his brother some kids threatened to beat him up. His brother instructed Robert to leave the house and not return until he beat those kids up.

"Beat their asses," his brother said. "Or I'll beat yours."

Robert returned victorious. It was just one more violent experience which made him very tough. That toughness would serve him well a couple years later, when he was sentenced to serve two years in a Georgia State Penitentiary for reckless homicide. At seventeen, while he was drunk, Robert was drag racing his Ford Mustang against another car on Peach Orchard Road in Augusta. Robert won the race, but ran a red light and broadsided another car with a young family in it. The mother and father in the other car were killed instantly and all three children ended up in the hospital in intensive care. This occurred after the "get tough on drunk driving" laws had passed, so Robert was tried as an adult. He did his time.

Later, in 1984, I visited Robert during a trip back to Georgia. I remember trying to hold back the emotions while he described his experience in prison. The prison he attended experienced racial riots on a regular basis – flesh on flesh, blood and bruises. Robert said that he had developed almost a sixth sense which would warn him when a riot was about to start. He knew exactly when to put on his boots to get ready for the coming fight.

Not surprisingly, his first couple of months in prison were the worst. He made the mistake of loaning another inmate five dollars. He soon heard that that inmate was telling other inmates that Robert was going to be his new bitch (I will let your imagination fill in the details on what this meant). Robert knew he had to stop this immediately or he would not survive the two years. The next day, Robert broke a chair over the head of the other inmate in the prison lunch room. As a result, that inmate ended up in a coma for several months and Robert ended up in solitary confinement, but he survived prison, at least physically.

Mentally, Robert was a mess. For example, after coming home from prison, Robert could not go to shopping malls or any place with too many people. He had developed a reflex which caused him to automatically strike people who approached him from behind. This reflex helped him stay alive in prison, but on the outside it was nothing more than a ticket back to the Big House.

Robert Hartness was tough and he was not going to let me, his best friend, hunt Jake down alone. Robert was only fifteen years old in the fall of 1979, but he was a scrapper like me. Surprisingly, a completely unexpected event occurred that night, an event which prevented us from starting our hunt for Jake. Even though it would not have been apparent to an outside observer, I was already deep into a spiritual transformation at this time. Despite my long hair, skinny body, fast car, drugs, guns, and threatening eyes, was changing.

Several enlightening events had occurred in my mind and life over the last six months which were starting to transform me. For example, the previous summer I had resolved to quit stealing. The boy who had been arrested for shoplifting three times before he was 10, the boy who started stealing from family before the age of 7, the boy who could not go into a store at 11 without stealing something, had resolved to quit stealing. This night in Apple Valley, two events would occur which would advance that transformation.

The first event was started by something that was most unexpected for the circumstances. It started when I decided to say a prayer. Can you believe it? With adrenaline in my veins, revenge in my thoughts, meth and MDA in my brain, and a gun on the table, I decided to pray. I decided to pray just minutes after I had taken the drug cocktail. Part of the reason the prayer was unexpected, even to me, was the fact that I was not a religious guy. I had run away from my father's home in

Georgia a year before, at 15, could not remember the last time I had set foot in a church, was not raised in a particularly religious home, and did not normally think of God or pray to anything.

Despite this history, something prompted me to pray. I did not get on my knees; I did not fold my arms. I may not have closed my eyes. I don't remember. The prayer was silent. The AC hummed. I listened as the familiar noises in the house washed away from me and I was left alone, inside my own head, conversing with the Almighty, wherever he was.

I just sat there, not telling anyone what was going on. I sure did not want the other people in the room to see that I was praying. I was the gun-totting drug dealer who scared really tough guys like Ellery!

The prayer was simple. It went something like this, "God, you know my heart. You know I do not want to hurt Jake. (This was true even then – I never found joy in violence). But Jake has ripped me off. You know I live in a neighborhood where I cannot let someone rip me off and do nothing about it. This neighborhood requires meanness to survive. Please help me find a way out of this. I am going to wait one hour before I leave to find Jake. Please help me."

I sat there for an hour, stoic. I watched the gun on the table. It watched me back. At the end of the hour, I picked up the gun, turned off the light, and Robert and I headed for the door. As we approached the door, we were interrupted by the phone. I walked back to the kitchen and answered it.

"Hey, man, its Jake," the voice said.

"Just the guy I was looking for."

"Look, man, I got robbed in there. Some guys beat me up and took the cash and threw me out the back door. I didn't want to come around the house back to you car. I was scared you'd shoot me. I wanted to give you time to cool off."

"Cool off? Cool off! I've been sitting at the table staring at my GUN for the past hour thinking of how it's going to feel when I blow you away!"

"Good God, man, please..."

"I don't want to do it either, Jake, but you took off with my cash."

"Please... I'm sorry. It wasn't my fault."

Jake insisted that he would never do anything to cross me. To prove he was sorry and to show his respect, Jake said he would bring his car to my house the next day (he had evidently located it by now) and leave it with me until he could pay me back. We hung up.

I am not sure if you believe in spiritual interventions, but I now do. I believe this was an answer to my unexpected prayer. There are three facts which convince me of this. First, Jake was not from my neighborhood and none of my other neighborhood friends knew him very well. I met him at a bar somewhere several weeks before and brought him into my circle of friends. I didn't know where he lived, and had no idea where to look to hunt him down that night. I did not even have his phone number. Robert and I were still determined to hunt him down, but we probably would not have found him. Because we did not know where to find Jake, he really had nothing to fear. I believe he knew that as well. Second, Jake was several years older than me and was simply meaner, having been exposed to even more violence than me. I do not believe Jake was afraid of me at all. Third, and most convincing, I never saw Jake again in my life. He never brought me his car and we never spoke again. So, why did Jake call me? Even more specific, why did he call right when I was walking out my door, within the hour I requested in the prayer? I am convinced the unexpected call was a response to the prayer. I am convinced because I cannot identify any other reason why Jake would have called.

Regardless of why Jake called, his call was the perfect story that night for the other hoodlums in Apple Valley. With the good news, I called a couple of the people who had left my home, recounted Jake's apologetic phone call, and invited them to come back to party. I never needed much of an excuse to throw a party. This event clearly met the mark.

Several of my closest friends came back to the house. I had also run out of cocaine, so I decided to load the couple of friends into the Grand Prix and headed toward Waynesboro to try and find some coke.

* * *

While on the coke hunt, the next cascading event occurred.

While we were gone, a couple of the younger neighborhood kids broke into my home and stole my stereo. When I came back to the house, I was shocked. I was shocked by the fact that my stereo was stolen and shocked by the fact that the idiots who stole my stereo did not steal the gun that I left under one of the speakers. It was clearly the mark of an amateur.

When I entered the house, the gun was just laying on the bare floor, begging to be used. But this theft was different from the earlier experience with Jake. I was a king in this neighborhood, and I had several spies.

Within ten minutes I knew who had stolen my stereo, and I knew where the little thieves were hiding.

I was going to teach these boys a lesson. The lesson: Steal from me, and you will get hurt – steal from me, and I will make you remember that there will be consequences. By now the cocaine, the drug of total paranoia, was seething in my brain. As I pondered what weapon I should take, another unexpected thing happened. I do not know what to call it other than The Voice of Inspiration. This voice spoke directly to my mind.

The thoughts which came to my mind were pre-packaged from an external source. This was clearly not my own mind making logical connections between ideas. Some unknown intelligent force was giving me advice. In this case, the Voice of Inspiration was a dialogue with that other intelligence.

The Voice said, "You used to steal."

"Yes," I responded. "But I have overcome that weakness."

The Voice said "Yes, and you considered it a moral victory. You looked upon your thievery as some kind of mental illness that you developed the strength to overcome. You were proud of this achievement."

The Voice was right – I looked upon my long-term habit of stealing as a type of mental illness. The Voice was also right about the fact that I was proud I had overcome this nasty habit.

"That's right, I don't steal anymore. I haven't stolen anything for months," I said. "It shows how strong I am."

I would often brag about overcoming this weakness to friends. I viewed this change as an achievement. It was rare in my world for people to change for the positive.

I was taken back by what the Voice said next. The voice said, "Who are you that you should have a chance to overcome an illness like this, but these other kids cannot have that chance? You, the one that just overcame this same weakness a short time ago, are going to beat these kids up for stealing? You can have the chance to change, but they can't? Who are you?"

These questions hit me like a slap in the face. I had no response. Who was I that I could have the chance to overcome a weakness, but I could not allow the same chance for others? I was dumbfounded, I was humbled, and I was transformed. Because the Voice was right, I forgave those boys that night. They didn't know what they were doing. Perhaps one day they would change. I would give them that chance. And I have never looked back with regret.

*   *   *

What occurred next was one of the more confounding miracles of my life.

After that night, I was unable to purchase drugs for resale without being robbed. I was robbed eight times in a row. I was robbed by eight people who did not know each other, who lived in different parts of the state.

I was understandably shocked, but continued to try and purchase drugs to maintain my business. I was robbed each time, without fail. Before that night in Apple Valley, I had never been robbed during a drug transaction. Through several years of dealing drugs, probably at least a hundred transactions, I had never been robbed. After that night, I was robbed every time – every time!

Many months later, I gave up my ambition to be a drug dealer. I had lost every penny that I had and every penny any friend or family member would lend me. I gave up drug dealing because I had to. It was as if some power had decided my drug dealing days were over. And then, just like that, they were over. It was as if I had passed some test -- or failed it -- and as a result I would be precluded from ever being a drug dealer again. I am immensely grateful for those robberies – grateful I was pulled out of that horrific lifestyle.

This miracle confounded me for years. It confounded me because I could not identify the source. It truly felt like there was some power intervening in my life. It was impossible for me to believe that these occurrences were a coincidence. But, then, where did that power come from? In one night I changed from someone Ellery would not touch (the same Ellery that beat up anyone that operated on his turf) into a virtual pacifist. Maybe I hadn't seen it myself, but there had been a change. I had lost something, perhaps the darkness in my eyes. The change was monumental and noticeable to everyone. No one came right out and said it, but the robberies were evidence enough. I had lost my edge; my vengeful anger was gone.

The thing that confounded me the most: Where did this intervening power come from? If there are evil powers in the universe, surely those powers did not intervene to keep me from dealing drugs. Surely those powers would want me to continue with that dastardly work. I have a difficult time believing God intervened because I do not believe God will intervene in our lives unless we ask him to, and we have to ask him in faith. This is why God had not intervened in my previous successful efforts to buy and sell drugs and why he does not intervene in the lives of many other people who are engaged in that damnable business. In this case, I was desperately trying to stay in the drug trade. I was not asking for God's help. What power had intervened?

It was not until about 10 years ago that my wife provided an answer, which I now believe to be the truth. Over 15 years after the events of that night, my wife simply said, "You probably changed." I immediately knew she was right. This was the answer to a puzzle I had been trying to solve for over 15 years. Forgiving those boys in Apple Valley transformed me in a deep and fundamental way. Something changed inside me. Something changed that enabled other drug dealing types to know, at some subconscious level, that I was an easy victim.

They could rob me and I would do nothing about it. They were right. I had decided that night in Apple Valley that I would not use violence against people who had committed the same wrongs I had committed. I changed from a person Ellery would not touch, to a person who could not execute a large drug transaction without being robbed. Despite being robbed and losing all my money, I began to view it as a very positive change.

*　　*　　*

My decision to forgive those kids that night had transformed me. I am proud of that change and what it did to my life. Through research, I now understand some of the science behind that change. In fact, as I researched this topic, I became inspired by how our understanding of the power of the human mind has changed.

One hundred years ago, most experts on how the human mind worked did not believe that our thoughts or beliefs could change us. These scientists, particularly neurologists who studied the brain, believed that our brain was a black box that only responded to environmental forces beyond our control. Like other muscles in our body, they believed that our brain was simply a reflex organ. Most of us have had doctors test the reflexes in our knees and lower leg; when a doctor taps on a certain part of our knee with a rubber mallet, our leg moves. This is how they also viewed the brain. In part, the discovery of DNA and human genetics suggested that our brain, the control center of who we are, was rigid and hard to train.

Way back in 1895, Sir Charles Sherrington, who won the Nobel Prize in Physiology or Medicine, conducted several experiments that "proved" to the scientific world that our brain was primarily a reflex organ. Based on the results of these experiments, Sherrington was convinced *all* of our movement occurs in response to external stimulus. He believed that we move, not because our brains command it, but because our spinal reflexes keep us moving. Sherrington convinced most of the scientific world that his conclusions were correct. The scientific world believed him.

As a result of this perspective, scientists did not even care what went on inside the mind; our thoughts and beliefs simply did not matter. This view dominated neurology and psychology for nearly 80 years. Consequently, early psychologists, like Ivan Pavlov, Sigmund Freud, and B. F. Skinner focused their research on how human beings *responded* to external events or stimulus. Like most scientific progress, their research laid an important foundation. Their research began to open the curtains and help us understand the power of the mind.

Early research showed that external stimulus could change what appeared to be hard-wired biological processes. In one of his experiments, Ivan Pavlov proved he could get dogs to salivate by simply ringing a bell. Pavlov accomplished this little trick by ringing a bell each day before he fed the dogs. Later, ringing the bell would cause dogs to salivate without any food present.

This process is called classical conditioning and works on humans as well. This is why virtually all of us, who are a little older, have to use the bathroom after we brush our teeth at night. We were taught as kids to brush our teeth, use the bathroom, and get in bed. By following this pattern, over and over, we have trained our brain to link brushing our teeth at night with a trip the bathroom. The same cascade of brain-driven chemical processes does not occur when we brush our teeth in the morning. Our brains have learned to only associate teeth brushing at night with a trip to the toilet.

Another simple example: Many Europeans can't stand the taste of root beer. Why don't they like root beer? It turns out that a popular cough medicine in Europe tastes very much like root beer. Their brains have now associated the taste of root beer with being sick and taking medicine. Simple, classical conditioning prevents them from enjoying a harmless pleasure.

In the 1960's, psychologists began to challenge Sherrington's conclusions that our brain was only a reflex organ. These scientists began to identify evidence that proved that our thoughts and beliefs mattered. New research was conducted that showed that our thought and beliefs could change our behavior. More advanced experiments indicated that our actions can actually alter the behavior of the genes we pass on to our children. In short, by changing what we believe, we will change what we do, and by changing what we do we can change who we are: Mind to Muscle to Metamorphosis. By changing who we are, we also change how others interact with or respond to us.

The deeper the research went, the more we found out that our decisions, associated actions, even our beliefs can profoundly change the chemistry in our heads – Mind to Muscle to Metamorphosis. We have learned that negative emotions, such as fear and stress, not only make our bodies more susceptible to disease, but can actually cause disease.

One of the more profound and scientifically proven scenarios, in which our beliefs actually change our brain chemistry, is the Placebo Effect. A placebo is a fake drug, like a simple sugar pill, that a patient thinks is a real drug. Because patients think the placebo is a real drug, placebos often heal the patient just like the real drug would – mind over matter.

Because placebos work, doctors have used them for many years and still use them frequently today. A study of Danish doctors found that 48% had prescribed a placebo at least 10 times in the past year. A 2004 study, published in the British Medical Journal, showed that 60% of physicians in Israel used placebos in their medical practice. Based on the research of Dr. Herbert Benson, a Harvard trained heart doctor, 60–90% of diseases respond to placebos – even nasty diseases like angina pectoris (severe heart pain), asthma, herpes, and ulcers. Placebo effect studies have even shown that patients who thought they had cancer surgery were cured of their cancer, simply because they thought they had surgery.

Doctors and scientists have struggled to understand why the Placebo Effect works. Maybe the patients who supposedly benefited from placebos were not really sick in the first place. Or, maybe the "cure" was only in their heads and had no impact on the chemistry that makes our body work. Maybe they only believed they were cured. Can the placebo effect actually be real – can it really change the way our brain functions? Does our mind really have that much power over the DNA-driven chemistry in our bodies? More scientific studies had to be commissioned to answer this question. Those studies have since occurred, and the results are profound.

Using PET scans (a test using a machine that can measure changes in body chemistry) scientists have shown that patients taking placebo pain medication (fake pain pills) actually generate chemicals in their brain that eliminate pain naturally. The placebo pills cause the brain to generate natural pain relieving chemicals (endorphins), but only if the brain thinks the fake pill is a real pain reliever. We now have the scientific and chemical proof that our beliefs can modify our brain chemistry and heal us!

In another study, brain-imaging devices found that patients with depression showed changes in the same healing cerebral blood flow as the patients who took real anti-depressant medication. Other studies argue that up to 75% of the effectiveness of anti-depressant medication is due to the placebo-effect rather than the treatment itself.

On May 7, 2002, The Washington Post boldly proclaimed the following, "A new analysis has found that in the majority of trials conducted by drug companies in recent decades, sugar pills have done as well as—or better than—antidepressants. Companies have had to conduct numerous trials to get two that show a positive result, which is the Food and Drug Administration's minimum for approval. What's more, the sugar pills, or placebos, cause profound changes in the same areas of the brain affected by the medicines, according to research published last week... the makers of Prozac had to run five trials to obtain two that were positive, and the makers of Paxil and Zoloft had to run even more... When Leuchter compared the brain changes in patients on placebos, he was amazed to find that many of them had changes in the same parts of the brain that are thought to control important facets of mood... Once the trial was over and the patients who had been given placebos were told as much, they quickly deteriorated. People's belief in the power of antidepressants may explain why they do well on placebos..."

Our thoughts cannot only change our brain chemistry; they can control the external temperature of our bodies. In his research on how meditation impacts biological functions, Dr. Herbert Benson, mentioned above, has documented how Tibetan Monks control their body temperature through meditation.

In one study at a monastery in northern India, nearly naked Tibetan monks used their minds to generate enough body heat to dry soaked sheets in a nearly freezing room. Using a deep meditation technique called g Tum-mo, these monks sat in a room that was only 40 degrees Fahrenheit. After they were in a deep meditation state, other monks placed 3-by-6 foot sheets, soaked in 49-degree water, around the shoulders of the meditating monks. For untrained people, these conditions would produce uncontrollable shivering, dangerously low body temperatures, leading to potential death. Using the power of their minds, these monks generated enough body heat to dry the sheets in about an hour.

In the field of psychology, these discoveries created a new method of treatment called Cognitive Behavioral Therapy (CBT). A number of studies provide evidence that CBT is effective for the treatment of a variety of problems, including mood and eating disorders, anxiety, substance abuse, and several psychotic and personality disorders. The National Institute of Mental Health has spent millions of dollars testing if CBT works on several mental illnesses. Their tests have proven that it does.

The old physics believed the universe was driven by matter: pesky DNA-programmed genes pushing us around. The new biology tells us the universe is also governed by energy, and this energy can be purposely directed through our minds.

Partially in response to these discoveries, Lee Iacocca, the President and CEO who revived Chrysler in the 1980s, said "The greatest discovery of my generation is that human beings can alter their lives by altering their attitudes of mind."

What would happen if you focused your brain energy to bring about planned changes in your life? How might that effect what you become? How might that change your success and your contributions to humanity and the world?

*   *   *

How far can this brain training thing go? How much can you change your life, your future, and your impact on the world by simply training your brain?

If I could convince you that you could become world famous, rich, and highly accomplished through brain training, would you be interested? How about if I could persuade you that you would become a well known publisher and that you would also create three new inventions, one of which would dramatically change the lives of every household in America? Would that interest you?

Maybe your passion is science. What if I could assure you that you would create two new fields of science and also create two unrelated non-profit organizations which would have a profound impact on everyone in America? Would you be interested then?

If your passion is education, what if I could make you believe that you would become the founder of a highly respected university and would create a separate organization which would advance the study of science and that you would eventually be elected president of that organization? Would you then be interested in this brain training thing?

What if I could convince you that you would become a powerful political leader who would help establish a new country? Would that interest you? What if I could persuade you that you would later be elected to another organization which would help bring about the abolition of an evil atrocity, like slavery, and would create the hope that liberty and justice could be achieved for all? Could you be interested?

There is one man who achieved everything listed above. In addition, he learned to play the violin, harp, and guitar. But that person did not reach any of these achievements until he learned to train his brain, and through that training learned to control his actions. He learned to use his mind to change his behavior, to change his influence on others, and to change his life. That person was Benjamin Franklin.

What did Benjamin Franklin do and how did he do it? Around 1730, Franklin, being somewhat disappointed by the content of a Sunday sermon, embarked on a self-directed effort to achieve moral perfection. In his own words:

"I wish'd to live without committing any fault at any time; I would conquer all that either natural inclination, custom, or company might lead me into. As I knew, or thought I knew, what was right and wrong, I did not see why I might not always do the one and avoid the other."

With this objective in mind, Franklin proceeded to watch his words and actions with unparalleled determination to eliminate undesirable behaviors and increase good ones. What was his initial experience? As soon as he started, he became very discouraged. Why? Once he started tracking his words and behavior, he was shocked by the great number of weaknesses he exhibited, and by the frequency of their occurrence. In short, Franklin found out he was a normal human being.

He then concluded "that the mere speculative conviction that it was [in] our interest to be completely virtuous, was not sufficient to prevent our slipping; and that the contrary habits must be broken, and good ones acquired and established, before we can have any dependence on a steady, uniform rectitude of conduct." He discovered that just *wanting* moral perfection was not enough; he had to replace bad behavior with good habits.

Once Franklin understood that we cannot improve our character by simply wanting it to happen, he resolved to create a disciplined process through which he could track and, through force of will, mold his character through time. He set upon a path to change his *want* for moral perfection to a compelling *desire* – he turned his *want* into an imperative. The determination started in his mind, impacted his behavior, and changed who he became – Mind to Muscle to Metamorphosis.

His first challenge was to identify those characteristics which would accompany a person of high moral character. Through focused effort, he composed the following list of twelve virtues: Temperance, Silence, Order, Resolution, Frugality, Industry, Sincerity, Justice, Moderation, Cleanliness, Tranquility, and Chastity.

At first his list only contained twelve virtues, but a Quaker friend convinced him that other people thought Franklin was arrogant. Apparently, in disagreements Franklin was not just content in being right, but he was overbearing and insulting (none of us have that problem, do we?). The Quaker friend then provided several examples which convinced Franklin that his arrogance was decreasing his ability to effectively influence others. With this advice, Franklin added Humility to his list.

With these thirteen virtues identified, Franklin set out to master all of them. Knowing he would be overwhelmed if he tried to master all the virtues at once, he focused his attention on Temperance the first week, on Temperance and Silence the second week, on Temperance, Silence, and Order the third week, and so on through the thirteenth week. Because this thirteen week cycle equaled one quarter of a year he was able to repeat the cycle four times each year.

Franklin chose the order of the virtues carefully. Mastering Temperance, the first virtue, would help him master Silence, the second virtue. Mastering Order and Resolution, the third and fourth virtues, would help him master Frugality and Industry. The financial success and independence that would result from mastering Frugality and Industry would make it easier for him to master the remaining virtues.

To track his progress, Franklin created a journal to record each time he failed in exercising one of the virtues. He recorded his failures every night, hoping he would be encouraged by seeing fewer and fewer failures over time. He got what he expected. His failures decreased and his successes increased.

Franklin followed this program for so many years that he eventually made holes in the paper of the original journal. He would erase the marks made during a previous thirteen week period so that he could reuse the page for another thirteen week period. He eventually transferred the journal and virtues to the ivory leaves of a memorandum book, which allowed him to erase the failure marks with a wet sponge (he followed this program for a long time!). Eventually, he extended the thirteen week evaluation to a yearly evaluation. Ultimately, Franklin,"being employ'd in voyages and business abroad, with a multiplicity of affairs that interfered" had no more time to continue this process. Even in those later years, Franklin recognized the profound effect this transformation process had on his life. How do we know? Fifty years after he started his quest for moral perfection, he was still carrying the book with ivory pages everywhere he traveled – fifty years later!

We can also see, from the records of history, how this self-directed transformation process impacted Franklin's life and influence. Using dates, we can see the direct link between this process and his contributions. Franklin started his quest for moral excellence in 1730. Notice the dates associated with the following achievements:

- 1731 – he founded America's first library that allowed poor and middle-income people to borrow books
- 1732 – he started publishing "Poor Richards Almanac," which he published for fifteen years, producing 10,000 copies a year. The Almanac was translated into French three times
- 1736 – he created the first volunteer fire department in America
- 1737 – he invented an odometer while serving as Postmaster of Philadelphia
- 1742 – he invented the Franklin stove and gave it to the world for free (no patent, no dollars to Franklin)
- 1743 – he initiated the efforts that created the University of Pennsylvania
- 1743 – he founded the American Philosophical Society to advance scientific discovery and was later elected president of the Society
- 1749 – he invented the lightening rod, which brought into subjection the previously uncontrollable and frightening threat of lightening, and again chose not to patent it
- 1751 – he wrote a book that led to the creation of two major fields of science: electricity and meteorology
- 1752 – he performed his famous kite experiment and created the first urinary catheter
- 1757 – he founded the first American fire insurance company
- Between 1757 and 1760 – he invented bifocals and gave another invention to the world for free

- 1775 – he was elected to the Continental Congress
- 1776 – he signed the Declaration of Independence and stands alone as the only person to have signed all four of the documents which helped to create the United States including the Constitution
- 1779 – he was appointed Minister to France
- 1784 – he proposed Daylight Savings Time
- 1787 – he was elected president of the Pennsylvania Society for Promoting the Abolition of Slavery
- He charted the Gulf Stream during his many trips to Europe – one of the first people to do so

Benjamin Franklin is famous today, but was he famous in his day? This guy became so famous that French women, known world-wide for their dedication to fashion, started wearing bearskin hats because Franklin wore them! Now that's fame! Benjamin Franklin was truly a man of broad and significant achievements of which there is seemingly no end.

Was Benjamin Franklin destined to have this impact on humanity? Were his inventions programmed into his genes – into his DNA? Or, did Benjamin Franklin actively play a role in molding the talents that made him great? Benjamin Franklin was clearly very intelligent, but people of equal intelligence are born into this world every day. Benjamin Franklin became great because he committed himself to a path of greatness. He became great by using his mind to change his behavior, which changed his influence – Mind to Muscle to Metamorphosis.

But what if your obstacles are not character weaknesses? What if your obstacles are physical? For example, what if you are paralyzed from the waist down? Let me tell you about one of my best friends, Mike Maddox.

*   *   *

Mike and I met in January of 1981, shortly after both of us had joined the Church of Jesus Christ of Latter-day Saints (the Mormons). We became friends immediately, partially because we had frighteningly similar backgrounds. In fact, Mike's youth was even worse than mine. Mike's introduction into the world began with tragedy. His mother almost died a few days after he was born – not from medical complications at the time of the birth, but because she had to go to work the very next day. She worked as a waitress and almost bled to death because she did not have the time or money for proper post-birth healing.

This tragic beginning would be followed by years of instability, characterized by many moves between housing locations. Mike, the illegitimate child of parents who would never marry, would move with his mother over 15 times before he was 10.

During those early years he has memories of his mom being arrested. Like the time he was arrested with her when he was only six. He remembers eating oatmeal the next day, sitting behind the bars of the jail cell. This memory was more entertaining than traumatic, partially because there are worse memories which plague his mind. Like this one: driven by poverty and addiction, his mother sold Mike to his father for $400 when he was 10 years old. That's right; Mike's mother sold him to his father for $400. Mike lived with his father until he turned 13, only leaving because his father died from delirium tremens from alcohol withdrawal.

Mike then lived with an uncle for a little while, until he decided to run away because his uncle complained that Mike ate too much. Mike would move another six times before he was 18 years old. During one of those moves he lived with his grandfather. That experience added another tragic experience to a long list of tragedies. While Mike was living with him, his grandfather died from a form of bone cancer that required part of his arm to be amputated. Between his birth and his 18th birthday, Mike would move over 25 times. Like me, he does not have a simple answer to the question, "Where were you raised?"

Following our conversion to Mormonism, Mike and I decided to serve Mormon missions. Mike and I also shared another challenge. Because we did not have family that could provide financial support, we had to work to save the money to support ourselves on our missions.

Mike was well on his way to achieving this goal, until the fateful day of March 19th, 1983. The tragedy of that day, and its aftermath, would attempt to exceed the deprivations and misfortunes of his childhood. On March 19th, 1983, Mike Maddox wrecked his motorcycle and was hurled into a telephone pole at 45 miles per hour. As a result of the accident, Mike broke his leg, broke his shoulder, punctured a lung, tore his stomach open, and ended up with 50 stitches in his head. Even worse, Mike broke his neck and pulverized his spine. The damage to his spine would paralyze Mike from the waist down for the rest of his life.

Mike had every reason to give up. Who could blame him? His horrific childhood was almost beyond imagination, and now, just as he was beginning to LIVE, the world had been snatched away from him. There was no consolation prize for the neglect and abuse of his youth. Instead of walking the earth and spreading his religion, he would be bound to a chair for life.

But, Mike had dreams and he was not going to give them up. One of these dreams came from a spiritual promise. Mormons have the opportunity to receive something called a Patriarchal Blessing, similar to the blessing that Abraham gave to his sons, as recorded in the Old Testament. Mike had received his Patriarchal Blessing before the motorcycle accident. The blessing contained the prophetic statement that children would be born to him and that he would raise a family – not adopted, born to him!

Here are the events that made his dream, and the prophetic promise, a reality. It started with an incredibly bold move on Mike's part. While Mike was recovering from his accident in the hospital, he proposed to his sweetheart, Shirley. He actually proposed to Shirley from the Striker Frame. Because of the significant damage to his spine, Mike spent months in a Striker Frame, which is a bed designed with two cots that "sandwiched" him in the middle. Every couple of hours, despite the horrendous pain, the nurses had to flip the Striker Frame over, so that Mike would spend a couple of hours facing the floor, followed by a couple of hours facing the ceiling. To prevent further damage to his back and neck during the painful "flips," bolts were literally screwed into his skull.

From the cold steel rack of the Striker Frame, bolts and all, Mike proposed to Shirley. Against any rational process one could imagine, this angel of a girl said yes. Against the advice of her psychiatrists – Shirley also desperately wanted to have a large family – this angel of a girl said yes. Against the advice of doctors – the doctors were sure Mike would never be able to have children because he was paralyzed from the waist down – this angel of a girl said yes.

But promises in a hospital room are not enough to make a family. To make a family, against all of these odds, would take hard work, dedication, and faith.

To start with, Mike would have to acquire a skill, and with this skill he would need to find a job. Although it is not always a popular notion, Mormons try to work it out so that the mother does not have to work outside the home. The objective is to ensure that at least one parent is always at home to help nurture the children. Despite his physical limitations, this is the plan Mike and Shirley wanted to follow. Even in his wheelchair, even with all of the other physical challenges associated with his injuries, Mike was committed to acquiring a skill which would enable him to support a family. Determined to achieve this objective, Mike went back to school and became an electronic technician in 1985.

As a paraplegic, Mike could have lived on Social Security for the rest of his life, but he chose a path that enabled his dreams. With his new training, Mike was able to secure a position at the Warner Robbins Air Force Base.

His new position, however, led to another challenge. The Warner Robbins Air Force Base was located over one hour away from his home, which led to a two hour, round-trip commute. Even in his wheelchair, even with all of the other physical challenges associated with his injuries, Mike drove the two hours every workday for 13 years. That is, Mike commuted to Warner Robbins until he bought his first business.

While these are all miraculous demonstrations of human courage and commitment, at least they are to me, they do not compare to the crowning miracle. Mike and Shirley, with no medical intervention of any kind, would give natural birth. Against all the facts that were so carefully documented by the doctors – facts with details – Mike and Shirley would have children. Did I say children? Yes, not one child, but four – Mind to Muscle to Metamorphosis.

The miracles did not stop with their children. Mike knows something about childhood hardship. He knows something about loneliness and a loss of hope. In addition to giving birth to four children, and raising them, Mike and Shirley would help raise 15 additional boys from broken homes. I have never visited Mike without seeing one of these boys living in his home. Mike would also spend over 26 years as a youth leader in his church and in the Boy Scout program. Mike is a miracle on wheels.

Today, Mike Maddox still runs a DJ business – music was one of the passions of his youth that he has not lost. You can find out more about Mike's DJ business on his website at www. mikesdjsound.com. If you have a need for a DJ in the southeastern United States, consider calling Mike Maddox, the miracle on wheels. You might even get a chance to meet someone who knows how to use their mind to obtain their dreams.

*   *   *

In the fall of 1979, in the most unlikely environment, I made a decision to forgive.

Acting on this choice was not easy. I was surrounded by negative influences, forces that made me want to retaliate and exercise revenge on the two kids that stole my stereo. I had a reputation as a tough guy, a reputation that was required to maintain my drug-dealing business. Displaying any form of forgiveness would destroy this reputation.

Without knowing where it would take me, I knew forgiveness was the right path. Throwing caution to the wind, I decided to act on this realization. This decision transformed me and led to a metamorphosis that altered my entire life. Our thoughts and decisions can change us, but only if we act on them.

New insights into the flexibility and power of the human brain demonstrate that we do not have to be slaves to undesirable habits. Our beliefs can actually change our brain chemistry, which can change our desires and actions. A recent book "The Brain That Changes Itself: Stories of Personal Triumph from the Frontiers of Brain Science" by Norman Doidge, amplifies this message of hope. Doidge's book provides example after example of people who have overcome crippling handicaps by retraining their brain. The transformation which occurred in these people's lives followed the same pattern that I have outlined in the last chapter and in this one: Change your thinking, and then change your actions.

Benjamin Franklin became one of the most influential people in western civilization through a self-directed process of metamorphosis. In the first place, Franklin changed his thinking. Following this change, he took action based on a new plan. Franklin dedicated himself to this plan for nearly 50 years and literally transformed the world for millions. Through focused effort, and by changing his actions, Franklin became a legendary figure in world culture. Benjamin Franklin provides a persuasive model any of us can follow.

Most magical to me, Mike Maddox has become a force for good in the world, despite apparently insurmountable obstacles. Mike had every reason to give up and not pursue his dreams and the promise that he could have his own family. Mike's metamorphosis started with a determination to reach that dream, it started in his mind. But, as is always the case, Mike did not obtain victory without taking action. Victory is achieved by taking action and allowing that action to change us.

*   *   *

What does all of this mean for you? How can you apply this principle in your life? First: Do not let your current bad habits cripple your potential. You might even be able to break the shackles of physical disabilities which hold you down today. I had learning disabilities in kindergarten and the first grade which placed me in special education classes. When I decided to go to college, in my early twenties, my family discouraged me because of these limitations. I no longer even remember what those limitations were. I have retrained my brain in those areas and have eliminated those weaknesses from my life. You can do the same.

Another path to success is to start small. For example, if you have challenges keeping commitments to yourself, learn to get up in the morning the very second your alarm clock goes off. Do not use the snooze button. This simple act, repeated daily, will build personal discipline and provide strength for larger changes. Action like this will retrain your brain.

Something else to try: Pick one new good habit or virtue that you want to master and that you know will transform your life. For instance, you may want to learn how to control your anger or learn to listen more than you talk. Focus on that habit for six weeks and you will find that new, ennobling behaviors will replace old, limiting ones.

I am still sad I missed Robert Hartness' funeral. My pain is amplified when I think of several other close friends from my youth who have died. The sorrow has two sources: First, I simply miss them; second, I now know many of them could have transformed their lives and escaped early death. Like me, they could have found great happiness on this earth. While I have missed the opportunity to share these principles with Robert, I have gained the opportunity to share them with you.

You can change yourself any time you wish. You can achieve virtually any dream. When you start your journey of personal or organizational transformation remember this important Fourth Principle:

Principle #4: By changing your actions, you can change who you are – Mind to Muscle to Metamorphosis

CHAPTER FIVE

THE FIRE PRECEDES THE BLOOM

The thump from the engine of my Honda Accord was barely audible. It was late spring 1988 when my Accord rolled to a fatal stop on Highway 25, just outside of Waynesboro, Georgia. The humidity was thick and the forest flanking Highway 25 was dense. The locusts were singing an eerie chorus.

In retrospect, I guess I can't say that it was "my" Honda Accord. The Friendly Motors car dealership that sold it to me the previous year never actually owned the car in the first place. The day after the salesman "sold" me the car, the owner of the dealership died and his brother took all the money and fled to South America. Talk about good business etiquette...

Unfortunately, the title was never given to the bank that loaned me the money to buy the car. Friendly Motors never paid the original owner for the car. The cash I paid ended up in Mexico and the original owner naturally kept the title. The problem for me was this: the bank didn't care. They expected me to pay the monthly payment, even though THEY handed $9,000 to the car dealership without ever receiving the title. Later in life, I learned that banks are not supposed to release the cash without a title. I wish I had known that little fact then.

This Honda Accord was about as close to a negative possession as I could imagine. I did not legally own it, never would, but I still owed the bank $8,000. What made it even worse: an old girlfriend, still living far away in Palm Desert, California, had knocked out the rear window. Her legal first name was Tempest, and every time I looked at my missing rear window, I knew why.

Genius that I was, I used the license plate from my old truck on the Accord because the state wouldn't issue me a renewal. According to them, I did not legally own the car. Figures.

I have driven over 3,400 miles in the last seven days – from Palm Desert, California to Dallas, Texas to Miami, Florida and now to an unexpected stop in Waynesboro, Georgia.

Miles and miles of sign posts, forests, swamps, prairies, and mountains... 3,400 miles in seven days. It's a long story, but I had finagled a deal to pick up another car and some cash in Miami. Unfortunately, the car and the money were not in Miami. I cut my losses, shook my head, and continued riding the highway.

I headed up to Augusta, Georgia to see my father, who was dying of cancer. The Accord kicked the bucket 30 miles from my father's home. Except for the Honda Accord, which I knew I would never legally own, I only had one valuable possession left: a Minolta camera. The Minolta was worth several hundred dollars, enough to push me through the rest of this seemingly impossible journey.

I traded the Minolta for a tank of gas somewhere along the east coast of Florida on the way to Georgia. Because I was unable to pick up the money in Miami, I was now completely broke. My cousin Stephen, who I picked up in Dallas, was sitting next to me when the Accord died.

"This thing will be gone before tomorrow," he said.

"What if I put a rag in the window? Do they still tow cars with rags in the window?"

"What does a rag do?" he asked, somewhat indifferently.

"Doesn't it mean that the car is broken down? Don't the towing people have pity?"

"Towing people don't have pity," he said. "They gotta make their money like everyone else."

"Give me a break," I said, chuckling.

I stared at my pitiful vehicle. He was right: The car would be towed away before I could come back and get it the next day. The Georgia State Patrol assumed it was stolen. Their assessment would be partly right: I was the last person to drive the car and I did not own the car, even though I had paid over a grand.

I found out a couple of days later that the timing belt was broken and the valves were warped. My situation seemed to be deteriorating by the hour. The Accord is in bad shape: it has no owner and it will never run again. As the last driver of the car, I was in similar shape. I am 25 years old, my father is dying, I experienced a business failure the previous year, I have a potential bankruptcy to look forward to, and I have been strung out on crystal meth for 7 months straight.

Due to my total inability to sleep or eat (crystal meth murders both of these normal desires), if I lightly scratch my arm with my finger nail I get bruises that last over 24 hours. Because I have pushed myself to the limits after months of non-stop partying, I look like a nightmare.

After the Accord rolled to a stop, my cousin Stephen looked at me in disgust. "You look rough, man."

"I don't need to hear that," I said.

"I'm sorry, but you look like crap and someone has to tell you"

"Shut up. Just shut up and let me think..."

In addition to being broke, I was broken. I had dark circles around my eyes, fragile skin, a pale countenance, and no cash. How did I get to such a barren place? Again? The story of the painful journey that led me back to the gutter, and my recovery, helped me learn this important transformation principle: The Fire Precedes the Bloom.

*   *   *

That painful journey started with a lucky break...

In the spring of 1986 I managed to convince the director of admissions at Brigham Young University to let me enroll. He let me into the University even though I did not graduate from high school and had never taken an admission test like the ACT. I knew this was a lucky break, so I worked hard during the fall semester, earned straight As, and maintained a respectful relationship with my professors.

This looked good on paper, but a heavy burden was at the forefront of my mind. The money I had saved to attend BYU would only support me for two semesters, and then I would be broke, with no one to turn to. Because I had no meaningful source of family support, I had to work for all my money. Without any marketable skills, I could not make enough money to go to school and support myself, but I made too much money to qualify for government school aid.

To get myself out of this pitiful situation, I had a crazy idea. Looking back on that decision, with the wisdom that I have today, I am not sure why I thought the idea would work. Maybe getting into a university without graduating from high school and getting straight As in my first semester made me too cocky. Anyway, without any business experience, I decided to use my remaining savings to start a business.

Not surprisingly, the business failed. The failure is not a very exciting story, nor is it a very uncommon one. I was young, uneducated, inexperienced, and overly optimistic. A bright eyed, bushy tailed, and unskilled "genius" with a plan to take over the world. Or, at least, to make enough money to push my way through school.

Instead of starting Microsoft, I ended up blowing my remaining tuition money on a failed dream. There were no more coins in the piggy bank. In addition to losing my meager savings, I was now in debt. Even then, an uneducated punk could borrow money. I was now looking for a short-cut, a way to make a lot of money FAST. The question: How could I get out of debt and get back on track with my education? For months, my search for a path of hope was fruitless.

Suddenly, my big break arrived. I heard that the American Limousine company was recruiting young single Mormon men to work at Desert Springs, an exclusive resort in Palm Desert, California. The limousine company was recruiting Mormons from Utah because Mormons are usually honest and do not typically drink or smoke. They wanted clean-cut drivers to interact with their high-end clientele.

I took the bait and accepted the job. Shortly thereafter, I moved to Palm Desert. Because American Limousine had promised a high income, I signed a one-year lease for a condominium close to Desert Springs.

Like most short-cuts, this high paying dream job quickly dissolved into obscurity. The owner of the American Limousine Company was a crook. Before long, I was working long days and not coming close to making the kind of money I had been promised. In fact, because of exceptions in the California state law for limousine and taxi drivers, I was not even paid extra money for working overtime.

So, here I was, living in an expensive resort town making five bucks an hour and working for a crook. I was stuck in Palm Desert for what felt like an eternity. I had jumped the gun and signed the one-year lease on my condominium. So, in no uncertain terms, I told the owner of the American Limousine Company what I thought of him.

"Well, that's fine," he said snobbishly. He smiled like, "I don't give a..." and let me walk out the door.

I searched for a higher paying job and ended up working for Valley Caddy, an upper-end cab company in Palm Desert. We drove Cadillacs instead of conventional cabs. The owner, Bob Shiller, was thrilled. He was not used to hiring taxi drivers that had the integrity and work ethic of a returned Mormon missionary and who did not drink or smoke.

My first night on the job I earned more money than any other driver had earned in recallable memory.

"You're the best taxi driver I ever hired," Bob told me shortly after I began working for him. "I got a position open on the night shift. Night shift pays more. I don't know what your schedule is like, but it's certainly worth considering."

"Sure, man... I'll take it."

The night shift, in addition to paying more, gave me the opportunity to work on my stock market research, which I believed would lead to riches in my future. During the slow morning hours in the Valley Caddy dispatcher office, I became good friends with the night-time dispatcher, Mean Irene.

Mean Irene was probably in her late sixties. She could have passed for 79, easy. Just like her name implied, Mean Irene had had a hard life. She'd spent years in a motorcycle gang and had a daughter that was now dying of brain cancer. My life had also been hard. These similar paths led to an immediate emotional connection between Mean Irene and me.

Mean Irene, like most people who try to appear hard, had a soft inside. We became close. I recalled stories of my tumultuous youth while she talked about her present and past difficulties.

Sometimes we compared war stories.

"You know, Irene," I'd say, "it's hard to determine who had the worst childhood between the two of us."

She'd laugh, dragging on a long slim cigarette. "I don't think it really matters, kid. All that matters is that we're here now and that we're still fighting."

"I guess so," I'd say, and then I'd get a call for a pickup and be gone for an hour or more.

As our discussions went deeper, I attempted to convert Mean Irene to Mormonism. This failed. It didn't take long for Mean Irene to see that I was disillusioned with my religion. I was at a point in my life where my devotion was more mechanical than spiritual. I was in a state of advanced spiritual crisis and I was entering a spiritual void in which I would begin to question the very existence of God; that same God that I thought had helped me break my teenage madness.

My attempts to convert Mean Irene actually backfired. One night I asked Mean Irene for a favor. She responded to my request, and her response converted me to something she was strongly attached to.

It was a cool night and I was working, as usual, but Mean Irene had the night off. Between taxi fares I drove to her house in one of the company Caddys.

"Hey, Mean Irene," I called rapping on the door, "Can you help me out?"

Her daughter answered the door and told me that Mean Irene was asleep. She told me I could go back to her room and wake her up if I needed to. Her daughter knew Mean Irene and I were tight.

I walked down the hallway and tapped on her door.

"What is it?" she said, answering like something from *Tales of the Crypt*.

"I need a favor," I said. "I gotta drive to Utah tomorrow. I have a family crisis."

"Yeah, so?"

"So, I was wondering if you had any of that stuff…"

"What stuff?"

"The stuff you use to stay up all night. I don't know what it is, but I know you have been taking something."

"Come on in"

I entered her room, which was completely dark.

"Here," she said, removing something from her nightstand. It was a small bag with something in it. I didn't even ask what it was.

"Thanks," I said, and left.

When I got to my car, a frightening realization hit me. Mean Irene was addicted to crystal meth.

*　*　*

I stared at the white, shiny rocks and shook my head. Mean Irene had given me a whole gram, enough to make 10-15 people VERY high. I foolishly thought that I could take just a little bit to help me drive through the night. I was very, very wrong.

If I was not in a spiritual crisis I would not have been so naïve... but I was, so I took a little bit. Crystal meth is a highly enticing poison. Worse, it was an old friend of mine. I was heavily addicted to crystal meth before my spiritual transformation at 17.

After taking that "little bit" I could not part with the gram that I had been given. As often happens, that gram let to more grams and more grams. Pretty soon, crystal meth was again dominating and destroying my life.

Bob Shiller would later tell me that I changed from being the best taxi driver he had ever hired to being the worst. Seven months later, I had spent everything that I had managed to save and was both broke and broken. I was sitting on Highway 25, just outside of Waynesboro, Georgia, sped up and burnt out, bruised and crashed, a walking nightmare of a human being, something pulled from the scenes of a 1970's zombie movie.

My car was dead. I didn't really have anywhere to go. I decided to stay in Georgia for the remaining few months that my father had left to live. This was a good decision, right?

No. This was another fateful mistake. I was now in a complete spiritual collapse and, to make matters worse, I had a history of DEEP drug addictions in Georgia.

My old acquaintances were more than happy to help me feed those addictions. By the end of those couple months, I was also addicted to crack cocaine and had been arrested for possession of marijuana. Some "rest period" this had turned out to be...

I had been a highly religious person and knew the Bible well. I knew my fall was accurately described in the following verses in the New Testament:

> *For of whom a man is overcome,*
> *of the same is he brought in bondage.*
> *For if after they have escaped*
> *the pollutions of the world . . . ,*
> *they are again entangled therein,*
> *and overcome, the latter end is worse*
> *with them than the beginning. . .*
> *But it is happened unto them according*
> *to the true proverb.*
> *The dog is turned to his own vomit*
> *again;*
> *and the sow that was washed*
> *to her wallowing in the mire.*
> *—2ⁿᵈ Peter 2: 19-22*

I had consumed the proverbial vomit—the REAL vomit, for that matter—and was wallowing deeply in the mire.

After I hit rock bottom in Georgia, I realized that I did not want to be in this condition for the rest of my life. BUT, I also knew that I was heavily addicted to crystal meth and crack, and that a major transformation would be required to break the addiction.

Breaking my downward spiral seemed utterly impossible. No matter what I tried, my addictive personality got the best of me. I concluded that I needed to do two things. First, I had to give up drugs for the sake of my own life. I remembered my past, how I gave up drugs at age 17 through several spiritual miracles that were tied to my conversion to Mormonism.

This time I needed to give up drugs for myself, not for a religion. This time the change would not be through miracles, which very quickly removed the drug cravings from my teenage mind. This time the change would be slower, but hopefully more permanent.

The second thing I needed to do was find an environment that was free from the temptation of meth and crack. That was extremely important. I needed to get away from others who used my most enticing poisons.

At that time in my life, I could only think of one place that fit that criteria: Brigham Young University. BYU is not like many other universities in America. BYU has a strict moral code that you have to sign and follow if you want to stay in the school. The moral code includes things like no smoking, no alcohol, and no drugs. If you break the moral code, they will throw you out. For the most part, the moral code is followed.

I believed an environment like this could help me stifle my horrendous addictions. At BYU I would have to overcome my destructive tendencies. Lucky for me, BYU had a policy that allowed students who dropped out with good grades to return without going through the admissions process. When I had left school I had good grades, so they let me back in without having to reapply. This was a fortunate break. I believed BYU would provide a wholesome environment where I could break my downward spiral. But, I didn't have the energy and commitment to get through the paperwork of a University enrollment process. I needed help desperately and I knew where I could get it.

*   *   *

My return to drugs had shaken my mother.

Although she was not a Mormon, she had every reason to believe my conversion to Mormonism, and my Mormon mission, had broken my early and severe patterns of self destruction and outright depraved addictions.

She had also substantially healed from the trauma of my youth. She was now emotionally ready to help me again. Because of her frugality and wise investments, she now had the money to help. Except for buying the suits for my mission, my mother provided minimal financial support to me after I turned 13 years old. She was a poor, single mother for much of my youth.

I also received little to no financial assistance from my father after I turned 15 years old. He had his own history of challenges. Shortly after his 16th birthday, he left home, lied about his age, and joined the Armed Forces. This was the time of World War II and my father was no stranger to the cruelties of war. Captured by the Japanese in the battle of Corregidor in 1942, my father experienced horrific atrocities during his three and half years as a Japanese POW. When he was liberated, at the end of the war, he only weighed 85 pounds, far below his normal weight of 190. Almost 80% of the Americans he knew during his imprisonment died. When he returned to the United States, after his liberation, he returned to the same unsupportive family that he left at the young age of 16.

Both of my parents came from tough backgrounds and did not have the resources to help me during my teens.

"I'm healing," I said to myself in my bedroom. I looked in the mirror. I had normal skin again; my hair was fuller and freshly washed. "This is IT. I'm on the right path..." In the wholesome environment of BYU, my craving for crystal meth and crack was gone in less than six months.

I learned a very important lesson through that experience. Moving to a healthier environment can help a person with deep drug addictions break those addictions.

I learned that this can even occur for someone with a very strong genetic disposition for addictive behavior. Along with other members of my family, I had a strong history of addictions that clearly had genetic roots.

* * *

Later in life, I learned that Dr. Bruce K. Alexander, a Canadian scientist, had conducted experiments that confirmed my experience. Alexander came up with the hypothesis for his experiments by watching other scientists conduct drug addiction research on rats.

Genetically speaking, rats have nervous systems that are very similar to human beings. Consequently, they are easily addicted to many of the same substances that we become addicted to, such as morphine, which is the addictive substance in the street drug heroin.

Studies show that rats addicted to morphine will do crazy things to feed their habit. For example, addicted rats will cross electrified plates to reach morphine dispensers. Their sensitive little paws will suffer to feed their cranial cravings, just as humans will put themselves through immense suffering to nurture a morphine dependency.

However, virtually all of these experiments are conducted on rats that are kept in small cages. The test rats are also often isolated from their furry friends. As you may know, rats are highly communal animals and prefer to live in packs. In his studies, Alexander concluded that the addictive behavior of the rats might be a function of the unnatural and isolated condition in the cages, instead of any specific genetic tendency. Maybe, Alexander thought, he too would spend his life sucking morphine water if he was stuck in a little cage alone.

To test his hypothesis, Alexander created Rat Park. Rat Park was a 200-square-foot housing colony for rats, 200 times the square foot of a standard laboratory cage. Alexander placed about 18 rats in Rat Park, of both sexes, provided an abundance of food, created private places for mating and giving birth, regulated the temperature, provided toys, included sweet-smelling cedar chips on the floor, and even painted the sides of Rat Park with trees, streams, and beaches.

In short, Alexander created "Rat Heaven."

Following the creation of this idyllic habitat, Alexander conducted identical tests on the rats in Rat Park which he had conducted on the rats kept in a typical laboratory cage. In his initial tests, Alexander provided both crystal-clear water and sweetened morphine water to the rats in both environments. He watched eagerly, wondering if the positive atmosphere would hamper the rat's desires to engage in destructive behavior.

While the rats in the cages quickly became addicted to the sweetened morphine brew, the rats in Rat Park abstained. He proved his initial theory: unnatural isolation contributed to, maybe even created, destructive tendencies.

In later tests, Alexander would go on to modify the experiment to further enhance his findings. First, he would get the rats in both environments addicted by providing ONLY morphine water for 57 days. After the rats were heavily addicted, he offered the rats in both environments clean water and the sweetened water that contained morphine. The rats in Rat Park actually weaned themselves off of the morphine, while the rats in the cages did not. Alexander again proved that stressed environmental conditions (small isolated cages) led to addictive behaviors in rats. Similarly, he found that idyllic environments do not.

Alexander had confirmed my experience. I too was able to break highly addictive behaviors by simply moving to a better environment – an environment with no drugs and new friends that did not use drugs.

*   *   *

I now call this transformation principle The Fire Precedes the Bloom.

This phrase applies because it describes what happens in mountain forests that are not allowed to evolve naturally. For many years in the United States, we attempted to extinguish all forest fires. The problem with these interventions: over time, without the forest fires, evergreens will completely dominate mountain forests. Because evergreens, like Lodgepole Pines, grow taller than most other trees, they block the sunlight from shorter plants. Evergreens also produce highly acidic needles. These potent needles fall to the forest floor and increase soil acidity, making it virtually impossible for other forest vegetation to grow. For these reasons, there are virtually no other plants in highly mature evergreen forests.

The way that nature rebalances this virtually sterile environment is through forest fires. Left to themselves, evergreen forests will burn down by natural causes. Lightening is a chief cause of these fires – as if the hammer of God descends into the forest and sets it ablaze for a divine change.

After the evergreen forests are burned down, many other plants are able to bloom, including beautiful flowers. Without the cleansing flame, the blooming flowers will not thrive. This analogy of the forest can often be applied in our lives. Sometimes the only way to create a wholesome and balanced environment is to destroy an unhealthy one.

Such is the case with evergreen forests, and such is often the case with us. The Fire Precedes the Bloom.

*   *   *

My decision to accept and take the crystal meth that Mean Irene gave me was partially caused by a string of stressful environmental factors: limited financial resources, a business failure, increased financial stress, a move to work with a dishonest employer, a spiritual crisis, separation from family, and an unwholesome environment. Most of the people that I transported in the cabs in the middle of the night in Palm Desert were intoxicated on one thing or another.

I am thoroughly convinced that I would have never turned back to meth if I had been living and working in a healthier environment with fewer stress factors. I am convinced of this because I was able to overcome these strong addictions, and heal myself, by moving to my own version of Rat Park. I have no craving to use meth and crack today. I am still living in Rat Park. Coincidence? I think not.

*　　*　　*

The environment is also a major factor in successful business transformations.

In the summer of 1994, while working for Ford Motor company, I participated in a business review of Budget Rent a Car. At that time, Budget was owned by Ford and was losing a lot of money. I was part of an assessment team that was sent in to evaluate what could be done to turn the business around.

Unfortunately, based on several factors, my team determined that the top leaders of the business were not providing the leadership required to successfully operate the business. Often, the root cause of business failures is poor executive leadership.

Sometimes, burning the forest means replacing the leadership. This was our recommendation and our recommendation was followed. While this may sound harsh, the wrong leaders can create an environment that is not only unhealthy for the workers in the business, and for the financial health of the business, but that is also unhealthy for them. Sometimes, the best thing for those leaders is a fresh start at another company or in a different job at the same company.

At Budget Rent a Car, we had to burn the leadership forest to make room for new leadership and a plan for business recovery. Most of the other business transformations that I have participated in included environmental changes of some kind. In some cases, we moved whole teams to new buildings in an effort to break bad habits and create good ones. In other cases, we have had to completely separate dysfunctional teams and forge new ones.

*   *   *

What about those of us who believe that we are not significantly affected by our environment? Many of us believe our strength to be so great that we do not let our environment impact us in major ways. We think that we are stronger than these mere external forces.

Here is a little test to see how accurate that perception might be: Would you be willing to administer potentially deadly electrical shocks to an innocent stranger if you were simply prompted to do so by an authority figure? Virtually all of us would respond with an emphatic "NO." This is what psychology experts used to think.

"No one would do anything like that," the doctors would say. And they were proven wrong. Through numerous psychology experiments, these experts now know that almost two thirds of us are willing to administer painful electric shocks to an individual if we are prompted to do so by an authority figure. Shocking, but true!

Based on repeated experiments, almost two thirds of us would administer potentially fatal electrical shocks to an innocent stranger because we were simply TOLD to do so by an authority figure. These experiments were conducted by the Harvard-trained psychologist Dr. Stanley Milgram. Understanding Dr. Milgram's research helps us understand the power that environmental influences can have on us.

Dr. Milgram was troubled and intrigued by the brutality that otherwise "normal" people were willing to inflict on others in Adolph Hitler's Nazi Germany. To better understand this chilling period of human history, Dr. Milgram conducted a series of psychology experiments to measure how people respond to authority, how many of us would have had the potential to be perfectly willing executioners in the Nazi-like atrocities.

Each experiment included three people, a Teacher, a Learner, and an Experimenter. The Experimenter and Learner both knew the true purpose of the experiment, but the Teacher did not. The Teacher was the subject of the experiment – the person who was being studied. The Teacher was told that the objective of the experiment was to see how punishment affected memory and learning. The real purpose of the experiment was to measure the willingness of the Teacher to obey an authority figure who instructed him/her to perform acts that conflicted with the Teacher's personal conscience.

The setup of the experiment was critical. The Learner was seated in one room with fake electrical leads attached to his body. Again, the Learner knew the true objective of the experiment and knew the electrical leads were fake. In the initial experiments, the Learner was played by a 47 year old Irish-American accountant trained to act for the role.

The Teacher was seated in an adjacent room, directly on the other side of the wall from the Learner. Thus, the Teacher could hear the Learner through the wall but could not see him. The Teacher was provided with an electro-shock generator that enabled him to administer electrical shocks to the Learner. The shocks were not real, but the Teacher did not know that. The Experimenter would stand right next to the Teacher. The Experimenter was played by a stern, impassive biology professor dressed in a white technician's coat. He was the enforcer, the figurative Nazi leadership.

The Teacher was then given a list of word pairs which he was to "teach" to the Learner. The Teacher began by reading the list of word pairs to the Learner. The Teacher would then read the first word of each pair and read four possible answers. The Learner would press a button to indicate his response. If the answer was incorrect, the Teacher would administer the fake electrical shock to the Learner, increasing the voltage after each wrong answer. If the answer was correct, the Teacher would read the next word pair. For the first wrong answer, the Teacher would administer a fake 45-volt shock, but would increase the voltage level with each wrong answer until it reached 450 volts. The electro-shock generator had a label at the 450-volt setting that read "Danger: Severe Shock".

After several sets of voltage increases above the starting level of 45 volts, the Learner would bang on the wall to indicate discomfort and, in some cases, would complain about a heart condition. After banging on the wall several times, all responses from the Learner would cease. The most shocking piece of evidence came next: Even after the Learner no longer responded to questions, the Teacher was instructed to continue to increase the voltage level and administer the electrical shocks.

"No answer," the Teacher was told, "is considered an incorrect response."

What were the results of the experiment? Many Teachers stopped at 135 volts and questioned the purpose of the experiment. However, most Teachers continued after being assured that they would not be held responsible. If at any time the Teacher wanted to halt the experiment, the stern, white-coated Experiment would provide the following verbal promptings, in this order:

"Please continue."
"The experiment requires that you continue."
"It is absolutely essential that you continue."
"You have no other choice, you must go on."

How do you think most people responded? In the initial set of experiments, 26 of the 40 participants (65%) administered electrical shocks all the way to the 450-volt level. Surprisingly, none steadfastly refused to administer shocks under the 300-volt level. Because Milgram and his colleagues were so shocked by the high-level of conformity in the initial experiment, they repeated the experiment in 3 additional US cities and in 4 other countries. They experienced similar or higher levels of conformity in all of the other experiments. In Munich Germany, 85 percent of the subjects were obedient to the end. Even after the horrors of the Hitler regime, the conformity that led to Nazism was clearly persistent in Munich.

This experiment proves that environmental forces can drastically impact our willingness to conform to authority, at least for most of us.

*   *   *

To what degree does our environment affect who we "select" as our friends? Several psychology experiments have been conducted to study this very topic.

What do you think is the number one criteria that most people use to determine who they will become friends with at work and school: shared values, shared goals, similar personalities, opposite personalities, a common religion? If you selected any of these potential answers, you would be wrong. The greatest contributing factor that determines who most people will develop friendships with at work and school is proximity. As a whole, in these two environments, we are more likely to become friends with the person who simply sits closest to us.

It turns out that most of us are not very judicious when we select friends in these two environments. We simply make friends with whoever is seated close to us.

Now that we know this fact, we might ask ourselves this question: to what extent have our friendships impacted our behavior and decisions, particularly when we were young? We can all agree that our friends have had both positive and negative influences on our lives. Consequently, we can change this impact by using more discriminating criteria for selecting the environments where we make friends. If we spend all of our free time drinking fermented concoctions in bars, that specific friend category will have an impact on who we become. If we choose to participate in other types of social environments, like book clubs, sports teams, humanitarian efforts, educational endeavors, etc., there is a long, long list of alternatives for most of us, we will be influenced by those people in different ways.

We can proactively choose our environment and have an impact on who becomes our friend. The question to ask yourself: Have you selected social environments that are going to help you reach your highest potential? Or, have you attached yourself to surroundings that feed your lowest cravings? Will your current social environments help you achieve your transformation goals? Or, as is all too common, will they create hurdles that will prevent your victory?

You have the power to change these influences. Take a powerful stance and start to become the master of your destiny. Take a close look at your life. Do you need to burn your social forest so that healthier relationships can bloom in the new space?

* * *

Another psychology experiment demonstrates the impact that others can have on our willingness to believe our own eyes.

In one study, designed and executed by renowned psychologist Solomon Asch, 76% of people will conform to the obviously incorrect statements of a group of people rather than defend what their own eyes tell them.

In this experiment, the subject was shown two pieces of paper. The first piece of paper had a single line on it. The second piece of paper had 3 lines on it, with one line clearly shorter than the line on the first piece of paper, one line clearly longer, and one line the exact same size as the line on the first piece of paper. In this experiment, the subject was simply asked which line on the second piece of paper was the same size as the line on the first piece of paper. But, as usual, there was a catch: The two pieces of paper were first given to eight other people at the same table. Those eight people would unanimously pick the wrong line on the second piece of paper. They were all previously instructed to unanimously select the wrong line.

What were the results of this experiment? 76% of the subjects would agree with the other eight people at least once. It was startling, but more than two thirds of the test subjects ignored what their eyes told them and followed the crowd.

Experiment after experiment demonstrated that environmental factors can affect us in profound ways. Rooms illuminated with red light lead us to underestimate time, while blue lights lead us to overestimate time. If we are asked to carry black boxes, we might complain that they are too heavy, while the same boxes, painted green, will seem lighter. Rooms painted red will make us work faster, but will also cause us to make more mistakes. Rooms painted red will also make us eat more. Thus proving an interesting link between color and appetite levels.

During the Middle Ages, Blackfriars Bridge in London, a gloomy black structure, was noted for its record number of suicides. Later, after the bridge was painted bright green, the reported cases of suicide jumpers all but stopped. Over and over again, we see that our environment can, in effect, control us.

*   *   *

What does all of this have to do with transformations?

Many transformations will require that we burn our current environmental forest to make room for a new life. Overcoming major personal addictions almost always requires that the person removes themselves from the environment where those addictions can be easily fed.

Many people have successfully overcome drug addictions by attending a resident drug treatment program, which removes them from access to the addictive substances and aids their victory. For this very reason, food addictions are often some of the hardest to overcome. They are hard to overcome because eating food is required for our survival. We cannot permanently remove food from our environment and survive. But, we can take actions to remove particularly addictive foods from our environment, such as foods with high levels of refined sugar.

My experience at Budget Rent a Car also taught me that successful business transformations often require that we make environmental changes. Transforming our environment is an important step to transforming our life. Whenever you embark on a journey of personal or organizational transformation remember this important Fifth Principle:

Principle #5: By transforming your environment, you can transform who you are. The Fire Precedes the Bloom

The Fire Precedes The Bloom

CHAPTER Six

REALITY SLICING

"I do not know what I may appear to the world; but to myself I seem to have been only like a boy playing on the seashore, and diverting myself in now and then finding a smoother pebble or a prettier shell than ordinary, whilst the great ocean of truth lay all undiscovered before me." Isaac Newton

The dark hardwood walls fit the overall character of this place. A strong smell of tobacco and alcohol fills the air. The dim light of the pub mingles with the darkness to create an atmosphere that make people want to drink too much and expose their deepest secrets. I no longer drink alcohol, but I have a secret that would shock my friends sitting next too me. I know if I share this secret, it will destroy the spirit of celebration that brought us together tonight.

It's late spring 1994 and I am inside Nick's English Hut, located in the center of the small university town of Bloomington, Indiana. There are several of us sitting at a table that's large enough for 10-12 people. I rub my hand across the heavily worn table top and can feel the grain of the partially exposed wood. When I look across the table, fond feelings warm my heart as my eyes move from one face to the next. Like the table top, some of the faces have also been worn by too many late nights. We have been through a hard journey together, a journey that forges loyalty and friendship, as we have struggled side-by-side through a challenging commitment. We are all about to finish our two-year masters program at the Indiana University School of Business.

I smile when I looked at my good friend Steve, who is sitting directly across from me. Steve almost dropped out during his first year at the school. Half way through his second semester he ran out of money. He had already received an eviction notice from his landlord because he had not paid the rent for several months. Steve was ready to quit and move on to who knows what. He had already packed all of his belongings when his parents decided to step in and help. They had disowned him in his early twenties because he had chosen a path that did not fit their view of the world. But now, he was working hard to get a masters degree in business. Time, the great healer, had softened their hearts so they stepped in to help. Steve was able to stay in school and struggled through the other demands of the program. In less than two weeks he will graduate. Steve is going to make it. I smile again.

Most of my friends at the table have a story or two that reflects the challenges of a program that demands all that you can give. I think back on how the journey was difficult for me as well. On one specific late-night study session, I remember looking down at my worn-out jeans and reminding myself I needed to buy a new pair. I had been reminding myself to buy a new pair of jeans for many weeks. But the curriculum was so demanding that I struggled to find even one hour to drive 2-3 miles to the nearest mall. I was grateful for my sweet wife, Suzy, who kept our kitchen cupboards stocked with food. At least I did not have to find time to buy groceries like several of my class mates did. I remembered another occasion when a dental filling fell out of one of my teeth, exposing an old cavity. Shots of pain would jolt my brain every time I drank a cold soda or ate a hot meal. Even with the pain, it was more than two weeks before I found time to visit a dentist.

Tonight, we are almost at the end of our journey and I can see the relief on several of my friends' faces, even in the dim light of Nick's English Hut. Earlier in the day we all passed one more hurdle that stood between us and graduation. Everyone at the table signed up for an advanced investment class this semester. For the final class project, each of us had to pick a stock investment and create a presentation that described why we chose it. This afternoon we had to present the results of several months of hard work. Each of us had to describe our stock selection to an investment committee. That committee bought stocks in a real investment portfolio that the business school managed, using our recommendations. Our entire grade for the class was based on today's presentation; several months of hard work were judged in a few short hours. To increase our interest in the assignment, the person who made the best presentation was awarded $1,000.

The presentations are now over and we can finally relax over a cold drink at Nick's English Hut. Dr. Renault said he would join us, but would be late. He is a very busy guy, but tonight he agreed to take time out of his demanding schedule to join us. We are all excited and look forward to rubbing shoulders with him.

Dr. Bob Renault is a highly respected international investment expert. Because of his extensive experience, he has taught classes and provided consulting services all over the world: in France, Venezuela, Poland, the Czech Republic, Hungary, Finland, Russia, Slovenia and South Korea. He even helped some of the Eastern European countries set up their stock markets after the fall of communism. Later, in 2003, he will be selected as the first dean of a new business school in Korea. Because of his international influence, he will also become the first Westerner to serve as a director of one of the major stock market exchanges in Asia.

For most people, spending the evening with Dr. Renault would not have been a big deal. It was a big deal for us. We just spent two hard years studying finance; but we knew success in this field depended more on who you knew than what you knew. We all wanted to know Dr. Renault and we wanted him to remember us.

*   *   *

Through the smoky light of the pub, Steve sees Dr. Renault enter the front door and waves his hand so that the professor can see where we are sitting. I watch Dr. Renault as he weaves through the crowded pub towards us. He approaches our table from the opposite corner from where I am sitting. I hope that he sits on the opposite corner, away from me. If he does, I won't have to worry about my secret, at least not tonight. But he doesn't. After saying hello and shaking the hands of my friends on the opposite side of the table, Dr. Renault comes all the way around the table, moves two chairs out of the way, and sits right next to me.

He shakes my hand.

"Congratulations, Kip" the professor says.

"Thank you, but it was really just a lucky break. Frankly, I am not sure how I won the contest."

"Don't be so modest" he says.

"Thank you again" I say, as I blush.

"You should invest the $1,000 award in the stock you recommended," he says. "I am sure the stock will do well."

"Thank you for the vote of confidence sir, but I need the money to pay some of my student loans."

Through luck and hard work, I won first place in the investment competition. Frankly, it was a narrow victory. Several other students did very well, so I am a little embarrassed to be the focus of the celebration; embarrassed, but happy to spend time with my friends.

I still wonder what my friends thought when Dr. Renault intentionally sat next to me. They could clearly see that he sat next to me on purpose. He went all the way around the table, and moved two chairs out of the way. I saw Steve raise his eyebrows at me from across the table when Renault shook my hand. I am sure my friends thought he sat next to me because I was the guest of honor tonight. I am quite sure he had different motives. I had already told Dr. Renault about my very lucky job offer. I had not yet told my friends. Many of them were still looking for a job, so I did not want to make them feel bad. I also kept the job offer a secret because it was shocking. The offer shocked me and I knew it would shock my friends. It might even make them feel worse about their job prospects, so I did not tell them about it.

I had received an offer to work directly for Richard Strong, a very successful investment icon. Not just a job offer to work in Richard Strong's company, but an offer to work directly with Mr. Strong, on his personal investment team. At that time, Mr. Strong was the CEO of Strong Capital Management, an exclusive and highly successful investment company that managed over 20 billion dollars of other people's money.

Getting an offer like this, right out of a second-tier graduate school, was a near miracle. It was kind of like getting an offer for a leading role in a Hollywood blockbuster right out of acting school. I was shocked, humbled, and speechless. My amazement made me hesitant to tell many people about the offer, but Renault was one of the few people I told. Dr. Renault knew enough about the world of big money to know that I had received a golden ticket to a very exclusive club.

The starting salary was only $50,000 a year plus bonuses, but, within a couple of years, the salary and bonuses could exceed one million dollars. This job was a doorway to riches, prestige, and some of my dreams – dreams that I worked very hard to achieve.

I am quite sure this is why Renault sat next to me. He knew I could become a big shot in a very private world; a world with lots of money, friendships with very rich people, and lots of meetings in rooms with dark wood walls.

The job offer was not the secret that I was trying to hide. The secret, that I did not know how to share, was even more surprising. At least it would have been to them.

My friends and classmates were all hoping that I would get a good investment job. They were good friends and I had their support. They knew I had dedicated much of my life over the last 5 years preparing for a job in the world of high finance. They knew I was a stock broker in my early 20s, which prompted me to pursue an education in investments. To add to my early experience as a stock broker, I had already completed an undergraduate degree in finance and would be getting my masters in a few weeks.

They also knew that I had invested over 3,000 hours of my time on nights and weekends doing investment research, without being paid. I often worked on that investment research, alone in my apartment, while my school friends enjoyed themselves at parties or Hoosier basketball games. I was completely committed to reaching my dream of a big investment job. And, now I had it!

My classmates also knew that I was getting ready to start an investment newsletter. I had studied the history of leading investment experts to see how they had started their careers. Many of them started with an investment newsletter, so I was going to publish my own. I offered my classmates a free, one-year subscription. Almost 120 students signed up for the letter. I was starting the newsletter, and spent 3,000 hours doing research, because I really wanted a job like the one Richard Strong offered me.

*   *   *

I think I insulted Dr. Renault. He was right to be insulted; I was ignoring him. But I was not snubbing him to be rude; I was ignoring him because I did not know how to tell him my secret. I felt guilty, almost disloyal, when I thought about the phone conversation from the previous day. That phone conversation haunted me. In fact, I stayed up all night thinking about it. Once again, sitting at the table in the pub, I repeated the dialogue from the phone call in my head. After talking to an executive secretary, I was connected directly to Mr. Strong.

"Good morning Kip, thank you for calling. Let me start by telling you how excited we are to have you join our firm."

"Thank you, Mr. Strong. I am actually calling about the offer," I stuttered.

"Is there a problem with the offer?" He asked.

"No, no problem with the offer. But, unfortunately, I am going to have to turn the offer down."

"Really, that's quite surprising." Mr. Strong responded. "You understand Kip that this is a very difficult business to get into, particularly for someone that is older, like you are."

"Thank you for your concern Mr. Strong. I appreciate your offer and know how lucky I am to have received it."

"Are you sure this is the decision you want to make? Do you want to think about it for another day?"

"No, I do not need another day. It is hard for me to explain, but this is the decision I have to make."

"I am disappointed. Of course, it will be easy to fill your position. There are several candidates that were hoping for the job. I wish you the best of luck."

When I hung up, I knew that Mr. Strong thought I was an idiot.

I could not bear to repeat this discussion, face-to-face, with Dr. Renault. He knew I had a golden ticket. He knew I was exceptionally lucky to get it. He knew I would not get an opportunity like this again.

How could I tell this world-renowned investment expert that I said no to Richard Strong? It would have been like telling the Queen of England that I did not want to be a knight. "No, your Highness, I do not want to be a knight. I will just continue to live in obscurity in the hut by the swamp."

I knew the professor was sitting next to me because of the offer I had received from Richard Strong. He was just trying to get to know me a little better. I did not feel comfortable maintaining the charade and I did not know how to tell him that I had turned the offer down. I could not find the words to describe why I made this decision. So, awkwardly, I ignored him. Maybe he thought I was being arrogant. I am not sure what he thought. What I do know is that he stood up, right in front of everyone, and moved to the other side of the table. He moved even though I was the guest of honor. After he moved, Steve raised his eyebrows again and slowly shook his head. Steve could see that I had offended the professor.

Another reason I did not talk to Renault is because I was afraid that he would tell me I was shutting this door of opportunity forever. He would have been right. By saying "No, thank you," to Richard Strong, I not only shut the door of opportunity to the exclusive money management world, but I bolted and sealed the door as well. By saying no to Mr. Strong, I flushed 3,000 hours of hard work down the toilet and walked away from the opportunity that I had been working towards for almost five years.

Why did I decline the offer from Richard Strong? I said no because of one of the more important principles that I now understand. I call that principle Reality Slicing.

*   *   *

The decision to turn down Richard Strong's offer was one of the most difficult of my life. The journey that helped me understand Reality Slicing was even more agonizing. That journey included a spiritual crisis that led to a dark void – a void where I would question the very existence of God.

That was the most distressing part of the experience: my growing doubt about God. I believed that God was connected to my transformation from a juvenile criminal. I worried that if my faith in God was weakened I might turn back to drugs. I believed that God, and my religion, pulled me out of a life of consuming addictions and crime. What would happen if I lost my faith? I was right to worry. As described in the last chapter, my declining faith contributed to the events that led me back to Meth and spiritual darkness.

In the chapter about Gisela, I described how our ideas can change us: by changing what we believe, we change who we are. We are primarily idea-driven life forms. My journey into the void of spiritual doubt started with a battle between two ideas. I clearly did not understand the true meaning of the first idea but I thought I understood the second one.

The first idea is described in the Bible. You can see it for yourself in the 5th verse of the 17th Chapter of Jeremiah in the Old Testament, which reads "Cursed be the man that trusteth in man." Similar statements are repeated in other books of scripture. This spiritual idea seems to say that we are cursed if we place our trust in other men. For me, the scripture also indicated that I could not trust myself – for I am a man. If I am cursed for putting my trust in man, surely I am cursed for putting trust in myself.

This idea tortured me. Why? Because we are idea-driven life forms – we are creatures of the mind. I believe that our mind is the mechanism that determines what we do and who we are. By changing our mind, we can change who we are. Consequently, not trusting myself really meant not trusting my mind

The second idea was one that I learned from the political philosopher Ayn Rand. Based on Rand's view of the universe, our mind should be our most cherished and important possession. According to her, "Man's mind is his basic means of survival – his only means of gaining knowledge." Ayn

Rand's view of the mind inspired me, and I accepted it.

Even before I fully understood Ayn Rand's view of the mind, and its apparent conflict with the scriptures, I was troubled by her wisdom. I was disturbed because Ayn Rand's insights into human nature were perceptive and profound; at least they were to me. This realization was distressing because she appeared profound and wise even though she was an atheist. This person that I was starting to follow did not even believe in God!

At this point in my development, the "word of God" was at the center of my understanding of life. I dropped out of high school in the 10th grade and spent the 7th, 8th, and 9th grades in a drug-induced stupor. I was on a dark and deadly road until several spiritual experiences transformed me. These miracles turned me away from crippling drug addictions and a life of crime. I was redirected to a path of sobriety dedicated to blessing the lives of others, and my own life, through spiritual works. I was redirected through the word of God. Those words told me that I should serve a full-time Mormon mission, so I did. To pay for that 18-month mission, I worked hard construction for two years and saved every extra penny. My life was centered around the word of God.

With my God-centered perspective, it was difficult for me to believe that anyone could have profound insights into life and the universe, and also be an atheist. I believed that God was the source of all truth. Now, I was becoming intimately connected with an atheist philosopher who appeared to be a genius, and I respected her views. The more I came to understand the thoughts of Ayn Rand, the more conflicted I became. These mental conflicts increased because Ayn Rand was not just an atheist, she despised religion.

Based on her view of the world, religions had been using ideas to control people from the beginning of recorded history. To a large extent, I believe she is correct. According to her, one of the main ideas that religions use to control others was the concept that we cannot trust our mind. From Ayn Rand's perspective, if people believe they cannot trust their mind they look to others to guide their life. Ayn Rand believed that religions taught people to not trust their mind so that the leaders of those religions could control those people. She believed that religions had used this approach for centuries. I was very troubled by the possibility that her interpretation of history was correct and I thought I saw parallels in my own religion.

Despite my strong and deep religious beliefs, and my growing internal conflicts, I did not stop reading Ayn Rand's books. I like to believe I am a hunter for wisdom, and I found wisdom in her writings. Now I was facing a spiritual battle because of a conflict between two opposing ideas, and the idea I learned from Ayn Rand was winning the battle. I had concluded that I could not be religious unless I could trust my mind. After all, I needed my mind to read scripture and to interpret their meaning. I needed my mind to form the sentences of a prayer and to interpret any answers that I might receive to my prayers. If I had to choose between believing in a God, and an associated religion, and believing in my mind, then the choice was clear to me: I had to believe in my mind.

*   *   *

The battle between these two ideas raged in my mind for several years and almost destroyed my faith. My religious convictions were nearly conquered until I learned to understand a principle I call Reality Slicing.

What is Reality Slicing?

Think about the vastness of space. Astronomers estimate that there are at least 70 sextillion stars in the known universe and many astronomers believe there is "something" outside of the known universe! Seventy sextillion is a really big number; it's a 7 with 22 zeros behind it. It is equal to 230 billion times the 300 billion stars in our Milky Way galaxy. In other words, it is 230 billion Milky Way galaxies. The known universe is really, really big. Think about that for a moment.

Now reflect on the variety of insects on earth. Insects comprise the most diverse group of animals on our planet. How many species are there? No one knows. Estimates range from six million to tens of millions. One of the reasons no one knows: 90% of them have never been described. Reflect on that fact for a moment.

Now, contemplate the size of an atom. Atoms are the building blocks of physical objects, fluids, and gasses. Try to guess how many atoms are in a teaspoon of water. One teaspoon of water has 3 times as many atoms as the Atlantic Ocean has teaspoons of water, which is about 200 sextillion – a 2 with 23 zeros behind it. One teaspoon of water has 200 sextillion atoms! Atoms are really, really small. Think about that for a moment.

Consider the field of science that studies the concept that we call time – like the time that ticks away on a clock. The scientists that study time are called theoretical physicists. Some of these physicists have concluded that time does not exist at all; that time is just a man-made perception that exists in the human brain. Einstein was one of the physicists that was not convinced that time exists. I do not know if these scientists are correct about time, but from all of these examples, and infinitely more, I know the universe is a really vast and confounding place.

The great minds of history have long known this truth. Based on the quote at the beginning of the chapter, Isaac Newton did not believe that he knew very much of what nature has to teach us. Many think that Isaac Newton was the smartest man that has lived in recent history. His theories reshaped our entire perspective on how the universe worked. He was so brilliant that his theories on the laws of physics stood unchallenged for 300 years. Yet, he knew that he did not know very much. He was right.

Three hundred years later, Albert Einstein introduced a new set of theories called Quantum Mechanics. Like Newton's theories, Quantum Mechanics completely changed our understanding of the universe, again. Albert Einstein was another brilliant scientist. As a result of his discoveries, we learned that splitting an atom releases more energy than 500 tons of dynamite. This is what Einstein had to say about our understanding of the universe:

"We still do not know one thousandth of one percent of what nature has revealed to us." Like Isaac Newton, Einstein believed that we are only scratching the surface of what nature has to teach us.

Given the short period of time we live on this earth, if time even exists, even the most ambitious, the most energetic, and the most intelligent human beings among us will learn very little of what there is to know. There is just far too much to learn for any of us to understand very much. In addition, physicists know there are other dimensions to reality that we either cannot perceive or can only partially perceive. We do not even have the mental or physical tools to perceive all of "reality."

Because reality is so large and complex, as individuals we can only integrate very small slices of reality into our minds. This is what I call Reality Slicing. It is the principle that any given human being only perceives and integrates small slices of reality into their understanding of the universe. We can only comprehend small slivers of reality, like tiny slices of a huge pie.

I am now convinced that we can trust our minds – I know I trust mine. But even if we do trust our minds, and even if the ideas we form in our heads are 100% correct, which is rarely the case, we still only know very little about the universe and the vastness of reality. Even if our minds are highly effective, and even if our perceptions and concepts are highly accurate, we will only understand small slices of the universe. We just do not perceive very much of what there is to perceive!

*   *   *

If we can only comprehend small slices of reality, how can we make highly complicated decisions that might have a major impact in our lives and in the lives of those around us? If we accept the principle of Reality Slicing, and we are wise, we will seek the help of others when we have to make complex decisions: others who may know more about the factors related to that decision. Because everyone experiences life in unique ways, we each have different slices of reality in our heads. If we are wise, we will seek the slices of reality that others have, to expand our view of the universe. If we truly want to expand our understanding of truth, we will seek to add their slices of reality to ours and enlarge the piece of the pie that we can perceive. We will strive to see reality through the eyes and minds of others.

Many people have also learned that there is a higher power that can assist us in our pursuit for truth, understanding, and wise decisions. I have learned to rely on that power and it has helped me make very tough decisions – decisions where I could not possibly know all the important facts. This power is often called inspiration. I believe the power of inspiration is available to anyone who wants it, religious or not. My experience tells me that inspiration only demands one price. The price is simple: you have to follow the inspiration when you receive it. If you learn to follow it, even with very hard, gut-wrenching decisions, the power will grow within you.

This power is very different than the process that we call thinking. For example, when I think, I analyze different facts in my mind and use logic to make connections: if I know that A=B and B=D, then I can conclude that A=D. But my thinking is very prone to errors, mainly because I am often missing critical data points (in this example, what does C equal?).

When I am being influenced by inspiration, it is like a stream of intelligence that flows into my mind with completed thoughts and answers. For example, you may remember the experience I had in Apple Valley when I forgave the kids that stole my stereo. I forgave them because I was reminded that I had been a low-down dirty thief not very long before that night. I was reminded that I had been a thief for many years. I was reminded that I had looked upon my thieving behavior as a type of mental illness that I eventually developed the strength to overcome. I was reminded that I was proud of those changes and even bragged about them. I was then flat-out told that I was holding these kids to a higher standard than the one that I had held myself to. In the first place, the dialogue that occurred in my mind that night was not initiated by me. And the final conclusion was not something I reached through a process of logic.

I have come to believe that the origin of that source is not my mind, but some external intelligence that is communicating to my mind. I still require my mind to receive and interpret the stream of intelligence that comes from inspiration, but I do not believe that my mind is the source of the intelligence.

*   *   *

It was the power of inspiration that told me to reject the highly desired offer that I received from Richard Strong. It was one of the hardest decisions of my life, and I paid dearly for it, but I knew at the time that the decision was correct. I knew through the power of inspiration. I believed I was saying no to the opportunity of a life time, but I had learned to follow the light of inspiration. At the time I made the decision, I did not know specifically why I should not accept the offer; I just knew that I was not supposed to accept it. I did not use a process of logic to reach this decision; I was simply told that I should decline the offer. When I follow the guidance of inspiration, I often do not get any tangible proof that I made the right decision. I usually only get a sense of confirming peace.

It was not until I read the newspaper on May 21st, 2004, over 10 years later, that I received validation as to why I was inspired to decline Richard Strong's offer. On the front page of the Money section of USA today, in the largest letters on the page, in bold, was the following declaration:

Strong Capital, founder to pay $140M in settlement

When I read those words, located under a very large picture of Richard Strong, I received a powerful spiritual confirmation. I now knew why I was told to reject what appeared to be an offer of a lifetime.

In May 2004, Strong Capital Management was fined 115 million dollars for investment fraud. Richard Strong was personally fined an additional 60 million dollars, which he had to pay out of his own pocket. The total penalty was 175 million dollars: the $140 million in the bold print, plus $35 million in additional payments to customers.

Because of his abuses, Mr. Strong was also banned from working in the investment industry for life. Eliot Spitzer, the New York Attorney General who helped prosecute the case, and who later ran into his own ethical challenges, called Richard Strong's pattern of abuse "stark and enormously problematic." Because of his pattern of abuse, Richard Strong was penalized with one of the highest personal fines in the history of the investment industry.

On the day that I read about the fine in the paper, I received a strong spiritual confirmation that this was the reason why I was directed to decline the offer from Richard Strong in 1994. I do not want to appear like I am passing judgment on Richard Strong. Given my long history of big mistakes, I resist passing judgment on anyone. To be frank, I am sad to say that I am not sure I would have been able resist the temptations to be dishonest that tempted Richard Strong. I think my name could have been in the paper as well.

* * *

I have now resolved the conflict between trusting my mind and relying on inspiration. I do trust my mind, but my mind only sees very small slices of reality. To help direct my life, I use my mind to seek inspiration from a higher power. Inspiration guided me in the decision to decline the highly enticing offer from Richard Strong. It has also guided me in several other important decisions of my life. In many of those inspired decisions, including other major ones, I have later received tangible proof that the decision was correct. More often, I just get a sense of peace and tranquility. By joining the power of my mind with the power of inspiration, I have learned to see beyond the limitations created by the small slices of reality that my limited view of the universe offers me.

While my decision to decline the offer from Richard Strong was a very spiritual experience for me, you do not have to be religious to apply the principle of Reality Slicing. I use the principle every day in my professional life by seeking the help of others who may know more about a specific topic or issue than I do. While I may know a lot, I now clearly understand that many people know more than I do on most topics. Even with my college degrees, even after visiting nearly 200 cities in 22 countries on 4 continents, even after working in 31 roles for 41 companies in 22 industries, even after working for some of the most respected companies in the world, like

Hewlett-Packard, Ford, VodaFone, and the UnitedHealth Group, I seek the advice of others. I seek the advice of others because I do not know very much.

When I seek help from others, I often look for people who have very different perspectives than mine. The more diverse the background of the other person, the more likely I will get a view of reality that compliments my own and that is qualitatively different from what I see. People that are more like me, possess slices of reality that are more like the one that I already have. While those people make me feel better about what I believe today, because their opinions validate my own, they have less to offer me in my pursuit of greater wisdom. Using this approach has opened me up to inspiration from the most unlikely people.

Embracing Reality Slicing has led to another empowering transformation. I have given up the bad habit of pretending I know things that I have not yet had the opportunity to learn. What a relief it was to give up this burden. Because I now know that no one knows very much I am not ashamed by the fact that I do not know very much. This realization frees me to ask questions without feeling stupid. This is one of the most powerful and transforming ideas I have ever accepted. If you want to see if a new idea can change your life, try to believe in this one and see what happens.

An understanding of Reality Slicing has also significantly increased my tolerance towards others. I now understand that another person can reach conclusions that are completely opposed to mine, and they can reach those conclusions through a process of thought that is completely rational to them. They can reach these opposite conclusions because their experience has exposed them to different slices of reality. In some cases, both of us might be right, based on the different truths that we have been able to understand. I used to think that there was a contradiction between Any Rand's view that I should trust my mind and the admonition in the scriptures that I should not place too much trust in my limited view of reality. I used to believe that these principles could not both be true, but I have discovered that they are both true. If we open our mind, and spend some time trying to understand why we disagree with others, we are likely to expand our understanding of the world. In fact, we may have the most to gain from people who are most unlike us. As I accepted this principle, I became far more tolerant of diverse people and their opinions.

* * *

What does this principle have to do with transformations? At the most fundamental level, the principle of Reality Slicing has taught me that I need help. When I am managing a transformation, either personal or professional, I seek help. The larger the transformation, the more help I get. In the business transformations I have managed, the first thing I confirm is that I can get the help, or resources, required for success. In business, adequate resources refer to executive support, money, time, people, and expertise. I never pretend that I can successfully execute business transformations alone; I know I cannot. If I cannot get the help required to be successful, I decline the assignment.

The same principle applies to personal transformations. We need resources to be successful in our personal efforts to improve. One resource we always need is time. We often attempt to overcome some bad habit that we have been perfecting for years in a couple of days or a few short weeks. Because it takes time to nurture bad habits, it takes time to break them. Many studies have shown that it usually takes at least six weeks to break a bad habit. With highly addictive habits it will take more time. When you decide to start a transformation, professional or personal, make sure and give yourself time.

We also need help from others – particularly when we are attempting a major transformation, like conquering a long-term addiction to drugs, sex, food, or gambling. As discussed in the chapter on Burning Boats, you will be surprised by the number of people who will be happy to help. Many people love helping others change for the better. As described in that same chapter, communicating your transformation goals to people you respect can be a powerful tool that can change transformation "wants" into imperative "desires." Most of us can be motivated to change through peer pressure, particularly positive peer pressure from people we respect. In addition to sharing your transformation goals with people you respect, schedule recurring meetings with them so that you can report your successes in achieving your transformation goal. When you decide to start a transformation, professional or personal, make sure and get help from others. For big transformations, get as much help as you possibly can.

Some transformations will require that we turn to experts. At 17, I managed to overcome crippling drug addictions without turning to experts, but only because powerful spiritual forces were at work in my life, and even those forces were initiated by others. I know I could not have made those changes on my own. If I were attempting to overcome those same addictions today, I would turn to experts for help. Fortunately, the experts who specialize in these fields gain more insight into the causes and remedies for addictions every year. The knowledge and expertise in these areas is constantly growing. There are now experts in virtually every field of human addiction.

Learn the lesson of Reality Slicing and accept that none of us know everything; there is just way too much to know. Turn to experts, whenever and wherever you can. One of the characteristics that I often find in senior executives, like Chief Executive Officers, Chief Operating Officers, and Chief Financial Officers, is that they never hesitate to hire experts when they encounter difficult decisions or situations. If these people, some of the most educated and accomplished people in our society, need experts, how much more do we need experts to help us? Thanks to the publishing industry and the Internet, guidance from experts is sometimes only one book or one web page away. When you decide to start a transformation, professional or personal, make sure and get advice from experts.

Organizational transformations always take money and a shortage of funding is often the number one reason why these transformations fail. For example, the number one reason that new businesses fail is a shortage of cash. Anyone who has started a new business knows that it is a major act of transformation. When I am asked to lead a business transformation, one of the first things I evaluate is the company's financial resources and its willingness to apply those resources to the transformation effort. If adequate financial resources are not available and/or the organization is not willing to properly fund the transformation effort, I do not take the assignment.

Fortunately, for personal transformation efforts, many public and private organizations provide funding and resources that individuals often cannot afford on their own. Many times, these resources are provided by religious and other non-profit organizations for free. If you are embarking on a major personal transformation, find out how you can access these resources in your community. You will likely be surprised by the resources that are available. I spend many hours every month, on a volunteer basis, teaching people from disadvantaged backgrounds how to successfully transform their lives. When you decide to start a transformation, professional or personal, find these sources of support in your community.

There are some of us who are just determined to do things on our own, especially men. This characteristic usually prevents us from getting help, even when we really need it. We like to think that we can do it alone. I had this problem, particularly when I was young. Because I was emotionally abandoned at a very young age, I learned to rely on myself. While self-reliance can be a good quality, it is often the primary reason we do not seek help from others. Most religions call this characteristic pride. The primary reason pride, which is not the same as self esteem or self respect, is bad, is because it keeps us from getting the help we need. This obstacle is as common in very poor neighborhoods as it is in rich ones.

Look around you right now. Look at the objects in the room you are in. How many of those objects did you invent? How many could you have invented? We all enjoy the benefits of innovations that have been discovered by millions of people over a long period of time. Consider how many of these innovations you might discover if you had been born on an undeveloped secluded island. Most of us would be very lucky if we invented the wheel or the spoon. Few of us would have discovered electricity, the combustion potential of oil, or a jet engine. If most of the things that make our life better came from the creative contributions of others, why do we stubbornly think we can make major changes in our lives (which is personal innovation) on our own? On the topic of pride, remember the words of Benjamin Franklin "The person wrapped up in themselves makes a very small bundle."

Understanding the concept of Reality Slicing helped me learn to trust my mind *and* to learn that I need help. It specifically led me to turn down the highly desired, but morally dangerous, offer from Richard Strong, even though I desperately wanted to accept it. In my professional role as a transformation expert, I use the concept of Reality Slicing to get the resources to ensure success. I also apply this important principle in my personal transformation efforts. Whenever you embark on a journey of personal or organizational transformation remember this important sixth principle:

Principle #6: Do not make major changes in your life on your own, get resources to help you, such as time, people, experts, and sometimes money.

CHAPTER SEVEN

TRAGEDY AT THE ALTAR

The image of freshly pressed tuxedos brings fond memories to my mind. For others, it's the flowers, maybe the multi-layered cake, or the colorful symmetry of the bridesmaids, standing in reverent attention, like guards protecting a solemn monument. For the bride, it is often the image of a wedding dress. A symbol that she conjures up in her mind every time she sees a bridal magazine or other pictures that represent the dream of "happily ever after."

It's May 16, 1992 and we are gathered for a sacred ceremony. My family is gathered on the right side of the room. Amy's family is gathered on the left. We wait in anticipation of the arrival of the bride. Elliot is also waiting, nervously, anxiously, as he stands next to the minister and close to the mahogany altar.

Blossoms adorn the branches of the trees, which are dancing in the wind outside the chapel walls. I can hear the branches brushing up against the nearby windows, like so many fingers playing one of nature's countless songs. The spring blossoms contrast with the unseasonably cool weather. In an effort to battle the cool outside temperature, the furnace in the chapel has been turned up. I am a little warm in my tux and try to loosen the collar that is now strangling my neck. Sitting in the front row of the chapel, I can almost see beads of sweat forming on Elliot's forehead. I wonder, is his obvious nervousness a response to the heat or his anticipation of the pending rejection?

The music starts: da, da, da, da — da, da, da, da. Amy appears, as gorgeous as ever, her beautiful dress trailing behind her. Her grandfather, Spencer, takes her hand and gently places it on his arm. Together, grandfather and granddaughter, they take their steps towards Elliot and the pending vows. As Spencer and Amy start the procession, I turn my head and look at my sister Kay. I am not surprised by the tears that start to trickle down

Kay's rosy cheeks. Elliot, her oldest child, is getting married. Dave, Elliot's father, holds one arm tightly around Kay as tears begin to well up in his eyes.

The procession continues. Step by step, Amy and Spencer approach the altar. With every step they take the emotions in the room climb. I can feel the tension growing, particularly on the right side of the room.

Amy reaches the altar and Elliot takes her by the hand as Spencer gracefully steps away. The minister starts, his baritone voice hushing the audience. "Dearly beloved, we are gathered here today . . . ." The minister reaches the part of the vows where Elliot has to respond. Time stops for several seconds as my family wonders what he will say. Several seconds feel like an eternity when time has stopped. Elliot responds to the minister and to Amy: "I do." The minister proceeds "Amy, do you take Elliot to be your lawfully wedded husband to have and to hold . . ." Amy responds as we thought she would: "I do."

Now the tears are flowing from Amy's and Elliot's eyes as well. But these are different tears; these are tears of joy. From my family's perspective, the tragedy has been sealed. Despite pressure from most members of my family, these two young people, who we believe are far too young, proceeded with the marriage.

We are convinced this will be a short marriage and will bring sorrow to everyone. The statistics regarding teenage marriages project a hopeless future. The marriage will probably fail. Elliot is 17 and will drop out of high school to support his young family. At 18, we do not think that Amy brings enough maturity to the marriage to offset what we believe to be an immature husband. According to the statistics, 60% of teenage marriages fail within 5 years. My sister, who is earning her Ph.D. in Psychology and works in a counseling center, knows other statistics that increase her sorrow. She knows that many of the teenage marriages that do not end in divorce in 5 years (the other 40%) are often not healthy. In fact, few of them are.

Kay, Dave, and the rest of the family are convinced that a tragedy has occurred at the altar today. Amy's grandfather, Spencer, had to escort Amy down the aisle because her father refused to come to the wedding. Everyone thought Elliot and Amy were on the high road to heartache and failure.

The family pain is increased when we think about the opportunities that Elliot is walking away from. He was doing very well in school and was a promising athlete. We also know that Elliot will not serve the traditional Mormon mission when he turns 19. When the young couple said "I do," our hearts were broken and our dreams for Elliot's future were destroyed.

Sadly, at the time, we did not think about Amy much, and when we did, the thoughts were not kind. We knew Elliot was making his own decisions, Amy was not forcing him to get married, but maybe his decisions would have been different with another girl. Like many families in this situation, we wanted to believe that our child was not the instigator behind this poor decision, that we had raised him right.

Our anxiety grows as Elliot and Amy have several children, one right after the other. They ultimately have five children in seven years; five children before Elliot turns 24. Kay also knows the statistics related to this behavior of teenage couples. Many of these young couples have several children in a row. Some studies suggest that they do this in an attempt to shore up a failing marriage and a lack of maturity. If they are parents, they conclude that they must be adults. Many of the children from these marriages do not thrive. We now start to worry about the children as well – from our perspective, children of children.

As we continue to monitor Elliot and Amy, they surprise us. Without a high school diploma, Elliot is accepted into a reputable University. He keeps a full-time job and finishes his 4-year bachelor's degree, in a very challenging accounting program, in only 3 years. He amazes all of us when he earns a GPA of 3.8 in his university studies. By the time Elliot is 23, he is earning more money than anyone else in the family: $180,000 per year!

Today, more than 17 years later, Elliot and Amy are happily married, their children are doing very well, and Elliot continues to make more money than almost anyone else in the family. Using virtually any standard I can think of, Elliot and Amy are living the American dream. How were they able to overcome what appeared to be impossible odds and find happiness?

*   *   *

Professor Tom Gardner looked like he was carrying the world on his shoulders, and the weight was crushing him.

Why? This did not make sense to me. I first noticed this contradiction on a warm afternoon in the fall of 1986. Lightly gripping the steering wheel of my Toyota Corolla, I was driving down the street when I noticed Tom trudging down a nearby sidewalk. The sight of Dr. Gardner, weighed down by some unspeakable burden, shocked me. There were no clouds in the sky, nothing but golden rays of sun illuminating the orange, yellow, and rust colors of the autumn leaves. Nature was celebrating the success of summer more than it was beckoning the rest of winter. My emotions were in lock step with nature that day, but Tom was clearly troubled.

It was my first semester as a full-time university student. At the beginning of the semester, I was anxious. Would I be able to succeed? I was a high-school drop out and a former criminal – could I do this? On this day, my heart and mind answered that question with a confident YES! I was absorbing the autumn rays of the sunlight and accepting the rejuvenating message that nature was proclaiming. The birds were still singing, the grass was still green, and I was optimistic.

My positive outlook was jolted by the image of Tom Gardner, shoulders bent, a frown on his face, eyes devoid of enthusiasm for life. I could sense a profound contradiction in that image, but I could not put my finger on the source of the inconsistency.

Tom was the award-winning professor who taught the Honors Philosophy class that I was taking. He was the major reason I was optimistic about my ability to succeed as a university student. I signed up for Tom's class with some fear. It was an Honors class, which meant that it would be difficult, and the subject was Philosophy, which meant that it would be even harder. I was quite nervous for the first several weeks of class.

But Dr. Gardner transformed the notes written by the great thinkers of history into a symphony. Not only did Tom introduce me to some of the greatest philosophers: Aristotle, Plato, Buddha, John Locke, Descartes, . . . he made the introduction with style and finesse. With Tom holding my hand, even I could explore the world of these deep thinkers; even I could successfully understand some of their messages to the world. For me, Professor Gardner opened the door to the vastness of the human mind and its far-reaching potential.

Why did Tom always look like he was carrying the world on his shoulders? What was the source of the immense burden that he seemed destined to carry?

I was so impressed by Tom's class that I asked him if I could use his materials to teach a class at the Utah Correctional Facility for Young Men. He graciously agreed.

During that semester, I lived with my brother-in-law and sister, on the outskirts of Salt Lake City. Every time I drove to the University, located in the next valley, I would pass the Utah Correctional Facility for Young

Men. I knew that I was initially destined to live in a place like the prison, with its high guard towers, tall fences, barbed wire, disinfected steal, and echoing chambers. I had been in and out of facilities just like this several times. I knew what it felt like to live behind bars.

I drove to Brigham Young University several times a week and each time I passed the prison I would reflect on the miracles that had transformed my life. If it were not for those miracles, I knew that I would be living, or dying, in an institution like the Utah Correctional Facility for Young Men. Instead, I was now attending a university and even taking an honors philosophy class.

Each time I drove past the prison, I would wonder about the young inmates inside. Were they like my friend Robert Hartness, who stood beside me in very troubled times? If someone like Robert was in that prison, wasn't I obligated to try and help him get out? How could I drive by this prison several times a week and not take action to help? Was there anything I could share that could help them find their way out of a dark world with no illuminated exits? Professor Gardner's class enlightened my mind in a powerful and liberating way. He helped me see potential in myself that I had not previously imagined. Maybe the illuminating thoughts of philosophy, which Tom had so carefully organized, could help these young people as well.

I began to wonder if I could teach classes at the prison. Could I, a high-school dropout with minimal college training and a former criminal, teach classes at a prison? I pondered this question for several weeks. During the same weeks that I contemplated teaching in the prison, I was troubled by the apparent contradiction in Tom's appearance. My perplexity increased every time I saw him outside the class room. Now that I was looking, I saw Tom everywhere: walking on campus, walking from the campus to his home, sitting on a bench in the outside commons area, where students would also gather on warm days. Why did he look like he was carrying the world and why did the world that he was carrying seem so heavy? The deep wrinkles on his aged face suggested that he had been carrying this burden for years. I concluded that somewhere in Tom Gardner's elaborate personal philosophy was a dark spot, an idea that weighed him down, a perspective that erased smiles and furrowed brows. Could I find that dark spot?

Overall, the classes that I taught at the prison were well attended. I was surprised I was able to setup the class so easily. It was a medium security prison. Would they let a very young college student, with minimal training, into a medium security prison to teach classes? They did. So I took Tom's materials, modified them into a ten-day course and taught the classes once a week for ten weeks.

As I taught the classes, I also searched for the dark spot in the professor's view of the universe. Was it in the materials that I modified for the first class, An Overview of Western Philosophy? I was not able to find it. Was it in the materials for the second class, The Structure of Human Thought? It did not appear to be there either. So I continued to teach the classes, and I continued my search. Eventually, I found the dark idea. As luck would have it, I did not find the sinister idea until the last class: Great Thoughts for Our Time.

Once I found it, I understood why it was so hard to identify. This idea has been taught for centuries and many people accepted it as true. I also understood why Tom accepted it. This ancient idea fit nicely into Tom Gardner's religion. Tom had clearly accepted this idea and made it a centerpiece of his personal morality. In fact, he reworded the idea into a phrase that he was proud of; he turned the idea into a quote, authored by him.

In the materials that I used to teach the last class, Great Thoughts for Our Time, I found Tom's quote. He had listed his quote with many of his other favorite quotes from other great thinkers. There it was, right next to this quote from Plato "We can easily forgive a child who is afraid of the dark; the real tragedy of life is when men are afraid of the light." Professor Gardner was clearly proud of his own quote and had used the idea to guide his life. It was crystal clear to me that this idea, enthroned by his quote, was weighing Tom down – even in the celebrating sunlight of a warm fall day, with birds singing over green grass.

*   *   *

Could I find other people in history that had tried to use Professor Gardner's dark idea to guide their life? Maybe even somebody famous? Could I find someone who had discovered why the idea was destructive and learned to reject it? I searched the records of history. I found the perfect example in the life of Abraham Lincoln. Later in this chapter, I give examples of how Lincoln followed the spirit of Professor Gardner's quote when he was young. But he learned why the idea was bad. Through a painful experience, he changed. In fact, Lincoln mastered the opposite of the dark idea, as demonstrated by several experiences before, during, and after the Civil War. One of those experiences involved Edwin M. Stanton.

Stanton was a confident and determined man. Born exactly one week before Christmas in 1814, he would become an important figure in American history. Eventually, Lincoln would enlist Stanton to lead the Union army during the Civil War. Many people were surprised that Lincoln pursued Stanton for this important role. They were surprised because Stanton was highly critical of Lincoln, both before Lincoln became president and after Lincoln occupied the Executive Mansion (now called the White House).

Stanton, a man of iron will, did not have the best social skills. He was the kind of man who could do virtually anything. But, he was also the kind of man who could seemingly do nothing without offending and insulting others. You know the type: strong, but hardheaded and with a sharp tongue. Stanton often said insulting things about Lincoln. For example, in a letter he wrote to General John A. Dix, soon after the beginning of the Civil War, he wrote: "No one can imagine the deplorable condition of this city [Washington D.C.], and the hazard of the government, who did not witness the weakness and panic of the administration, and the painful imbecility of Lincoln." Stanton even referred to Lincoln as the "Original Gorilla," suggesting that evolution had been unkind to the President, both in his ungainly appearance and in his weak intelligence. Even after Stanton was confirmed as Secretary of War, he often criticized Lincoln, the Commander in Chief, and was sometimes insubordinate.

In one incident, Illinois Congressman Owen Lovejoy convinced Lincoln to issue a Presidential Order to redeploy troops. When Lovejoy took the order to Stanton's office, Stanton flatly refused and stated:

"Lincoln is a damn fool for ever signing that order."

Shocked by Stanton's irreverent comment about the President, Lovejoy responded "Do you mean the President is a damned fool?"

"Yes sir," Stanton said, "if he gave you such an order as that."

Surprised by Stanton's insubordination, Lovejoy returned to the Executive Mansion and described Stanton's insolence to Lincoln. When Lovejoy had finished, Lincoln asked point blank:

"Did Stanton say I was a damned fool?"

Lovejoy was a congressman from the same state where Lincoln had practiced law for 23 years before he was elected to the presidency. Lovejoy had helped Lincoln win the election. Lovejoy was a friend. Not only had Stanton challenged Lincoln's presidential authority in front of Congressman Lovejoy, he did so with disrespect for the office and the President. He did so with disrespect for his close friend.

Lovejoy answered Lincoln's point blank question: "Yes."

How did Lincoln respond to this insult and insubordination? Almost 150 years later, Lincoln's response is often quoted with admiration and awe.

His response: "If Stanton said I was a damn fool, then I must be one, for he is nearly always right, and generally says what he means. I will step over and see him."

After consulting with Stanton, Lincoln not only supported his refusal to follow the order, Lincoln said the following about Stanton:

"Gentlemen, it is my duty to submit. I cannot add to Mr. Stanton's troubles. His position is one of the most difficult in the world. . . . The pressure upon him is immeasurable and unending. He is the rock on the beach of our national ocean against which the breakers dash and roar, dash and roar, without ceasing. He fights back the angry waters and prevents them from undermining and overwhelming the land. Gentlemen, I do not see how he survives, why he is not crushed and torn to pieces."

As a result of Lincoln's forgiving philosophy and reconciling responses to Stanton's harsh personality, Stanton eventually became one of Lincoln's strong supporters. So much so that after Lincoln's assassination, Stanton made these comments at Lincoln's grave:

"There lies the most perfect ruler of men the world has ever seen. Now he belongs to the ages."

Lincoln turned Stanton, a former staunch enemy, into a friend.

Lincoln's responses to Stanton were not unique. Lincoln approached many people this way during his presidential years. In his 1861 inaugural address, he passionately pleaded for friendship with the South.

"The Government will not assail you. You can have no conflict without being yourselves the aggressors. You have no oath registered in heaven to destroy the Government, while I shall have the most solemn one to preserve, protect, and defend it."

In his closing statements of that same inaugural address Lincoln said "We are *not enemies*, but *friends*. We *must not be enemies*."

Despite these gestures of peace, and other efforts of reconciliation from Lincoln, the Civil War began and raged for four years, killing 360,000 Americans.

Even after a bitter and deadly war, even after the North had clearly won, Lincoln continued to try to turn his southern enemies into friends. Shortly after the War, he hosted a dinner and invited several Confederate leaders from the South. Before the dinner, the President setup a reception line so that he could personally and warmly welcome Southern leaders to the dinner. Seeing Lincoln's behavior, a Northern woman approached Lincoln and said:

"Mr. President, These are your enemies. You shouldn't invite them to dinner, you should destroy them."

Lincoln smiled and replied, "Madam, don't I destroy my enemies when I make them my friends?"

Lincoln maintained this philosophy to the end of his days. At his last cabinet meeting, on the morning of the very day that he was assassinated, he responded to Northern demands to hang Southern leaders by stating:

"I hope there will be no persecution, no bloody work after the war is over. No one need expect me to take any part in hanging or killing these men....Enough lives have been sacrificed. We must extinguish our resentments if we expect harmony and union."

Lincoln had many passions, but one of his most admirable was his desire to destroy his enemies by turning them into friends.

*   *   *

How is this related to Tom Gardner? What was the idea that Tom accepted, which weighed him down on autumn days filled with rejuvenating sunshine? The concept will seem innocent to most and the peak of morality to some. The quote that Professor Gardner penned was this: "The duty of every servant of God is to relieve suffering."

Some of you are now shocked that I think this is a sinister idea. What is so bad about focusing your efforts on the relief of suffering? How could this be a dark idea and why would I make this discussion a central part of this chapter? It is dark because it focuses our energy on the elimination of something that is negative (suffering) instead of the creation of a something that is positive (happiness).

A great power will come into your life when you focus your energy, not on the elimination of negatives, but on the creation of positives. Instead of destroying enemies through conflict and violence, attempt to create friends through reconciliation. Instead of destroying criminals through penal institutions, help them transform into productive members of society through the power of human transformation. Instead of trying to lose weight prepare yourself to run a marathon. Learn to focus your energy on creating positives, instead of eliminating negatives, and your life will blossom.

Other inspiring personalities clearly understood the power of focusing on positive outcomes. Mother Teresa demonstrated her understanding of this idea when she refused to attend an anti-war rally. "If you have a peace rally," she said, "please invite me." Mother Teresa did not focus her energy on eliminating negatives.

Albert Einstein also understood this principle. On the same topic, war, Einstein said "You cannot simultaneously prevent and prepare for war." This was a particularly painful subject for him. Einstein learned first hand that when you prepare for war, you inevitably create new weapons. When you create new weapons, you usually end up using them. It was Einstein's genius that created the atom bomb. One of the greatest regrets of Einstein's life is that he discovered the scientific principles that created nuclear weapons. Maybe more than anyone who has ever lived, Einstein understood the danger that comes from focusing your energy on creating negatives.

Through my interactions with Tom Gardner, I learned why focusing our energy on eliminating negatives is not ideal. Dr. Gardner had set an impossible goal for himself, the elimination of suffering, and was weighed down by it. However, at that early stage of my life I did not fully understand the power that I could harness by focusing my energy on creating positives. I did not fully understand this power until I decided to figure out why my nephew Elliot was so successful. Frankly, at that time, Elliot was far more successful than me.

*   *   *

My family was surprised by Elliot's success. We were all happy for him, but also somewhat confounded. You probably have someone in your family with the Midas Touch; someone who seems to succeed at whatever they do. I was surprised as well, but I did not think about it much. That is, I did not think about it much until Elliot got a job, by accident, that I had worked really hard to get, without success.

In 1998, while working at Hewlett Packard (HP), I decided I wanted to make more money. My career at HP was going well and it was a great company to work for, but I believed I could do better. I lived in Silicon Valley and heard frequent stories of people multiplying their income by getting jobs in high-demand technologies. Jim Fortner, one of my friends and coworkers at HP, left the company in 1997 to work in a new and exciting area. He had some crazy ideas about building business software that would work on the World Wide Web. Jim tripled his income in one year.

I was a mid-level corporate manager with a masters degree in business. I had learned how to analyze market trends. I had the skills to identify high-demand technologies. I decided I would follow Jim's example. I analyzed the market, spent hours doing the research, and identified a growing opportunity.

As a result of that research, I decided to become an SAP consultant (SAP is a software system that big companies use to run large parts of their business). I identified the leading companies that hired SAP consultants, I bought SAP books and studied them, and I polished up my resume. I remember working late nights and weekends preparing for this career change. After I was prepared, I started my job hunt. I sent my resume to everyone that was looking for SAP consultants. I got several interviews, but never received an offer. I was very disappointed.

About the same time, Elliot was working as an accounting auditor in Phoenix. He and

Amy decided that they wanted to move back to Utah to be near family. Elliot's dad helped him get a job as a Cobol software programmer at the headquarters for the Albertson's grocery store chain. Frankly, he was very lucky to get this job, because Elliot had no formal training as a software engineer.

The day before Elliot was supposed to start at Albertsons he was asked to interview for a software programmer position at another company. That company gave Elliot a job offer right on the spot. Later in the day, he called me and asked me which job he should take. Guess what the other job was? It was an SAP job! I told him to take it and continued to look for an SAP job myself.

I was 10 years older, I had more education, I had more experience, and I was just as motivated, probably just as smart. Through careful research, I identified SAP as a growing market. I studied SAP books. I identified companies that hired SAP consultants. I did everything I knew how to do but never did get an SAP job. Elliot got an SAP job without even knowing what it was. It fell into his lap.

I licked my wounds and blew the experience off as bad luck. But I started to watch Elliot more closely. Was it a coincidence that this huge opportunity fell into his lap? Or, did he know something about success that I did not know? Did he do something that I did not know how to do? As I watched Elliot's continued success, I became convinced that he had some secret. I was determined to learn his secret.

After thinking about it for several months, I called Elliot to discover his secret. I had to humble myself to make the call. I was the uncle and was 10 years older; I shouldn't have to call my nephew for career advice. I remember the day very clearly. It was a Saturday and the sun was shining. Despite my reservations, I was excited. I thought I was about to learn the secret that would change my professional career. Guess what Elliot's response was? Elliot was completely surprised by the call. He did not believe that he had any secret at all.

Despite his initial response, I did not give up. I asked him if we could continue to talk about what made him so successful. I could picture his smiling face on the other side of the phone when he said yes.

After multiple phone calls (we did not live in the same state) I developed a two-part theory. First, Elliot simply believed that good things would happen to him; he simply believed that he would be successful, so he was. Second, Elliot seemed to respond to failure better than others. We all experience failure, but we do not all respond in the same way. Some people let failures devastate them and they quit. Others see failures as a temporary nuisance, a brief distraction on their path to glory. Elliot fell into the latter category. He did not let unexpected challenges in his life stop him from reaching his dreams.

I was convinced that this last part of the theory was Elliot's secret formula for success. I wondered: had anyone studied this aspect of human psychology? Had anyone studied how people respond to failure and how their responses impacted their level of success? Could I find research that confirmed my theory about Elliot? More importantly, could I learn this skill? Could I change how I responded to failure and achieve higher levels of success? With these questions, I began my search for answers. That search led me to Martin E. P. Seligman, Ph. D.

*   *   *

Many people view Dr. Seligman as the founder of the science of Positive Psychology. He has led, designed, or inspired multiple studies that measure how people respond to success and failure. His research proves that the way we explain our accomplishments or setbacks to ourselves makes a difference. In fact, the way we respond profoundly impacts the level of success we will experience. But he did not focus his research on the factors that lead to success until a very important plane trip. That plane trip completely changed the direction of his work.

In 1982, nearly 15 years after Martin Seligman started his career, he was flying across the country, from San Francisco to Philadelphia. He settled into his seat, buckled his seat belt, and hoped for a quiet flight. It was a long flight and he needed the rest. His hopes for solitude were dashed when John Leslie, the gentleman sitting next to him, forced a conversation. Leslie began telling Seligman about some of the most successful teams that he managed and how these teams believed that they could walk on water. The conversation intrigued Seligman.

Leslie then asked Seligman what he did. Seligman outlined his extensive research on a topic he called Learned Helplessness. He described experiments that showed how rats, who were afflicted by environmental factors that they could not control (like electrical shocks or high-pitched sounds), developed learned helplessness. These rats demonstrated all the classic signs of depression. Through additional studies, some of which focused on people, it was clear that learned helplessness and depression had the very same effects on human behavior. This was a big breakthrough. Because of this insight, the many years that Seligman and others had devoted to studying learned helplessness might provide a greater understanding of depression: its causes, its effects and, most importantly, potential cures.

The effects of learned helplessness, or depression, can be catastrophic. In one study, rats that had developed learned helplessness were 40% more likely to die from a given cancer than the control group (rats that were not subjected to the shocks and noises). Similar effects are observed in humans. Depression increases disease, lowers performance, and makes life miserable.

Dr. Seligman made another major breakthrough. He discovered that depression and pessimism are connected. Pessimists experienced depression more often and their episodes of depression lasted longer. Not a surprising discovery, but Seligman proved it through controlled research.

This breakthrough was followed by yet another big discovery. Seligman identified clear behavioral traits that measured if someone was a pessimist. These traits are related to how people describe failure in their life. He calls it their Explanatory Style. When pessimists fail, they often describe or explain the event as:

- Permanent – they will continue to fail in much the same way
- Pervasive – a failure in one part of their life will cause failures in other parts of their life. For example, if they lose their job, their marriage will likely fall apart, and
- Personal – the failure probably resulted from a personal limitation or weakness

Unfortunately, pessimists often tend to view success in the opposite way. They view it as temporary (this will not happen again), localized (the success will not lead to success in other parts of their life), and impersonal (the success had nothing to do with anything they did). Isn't it sad that, in general, pessimists take credit for their failures, but do not take credit for their successes? Because of this explanatory style, Seligman discovered that pessimists often quit trying when they face challenges. Who wouldn't quit if they believed that failures were permanent, pervasive, and personal!

Here is the great news: Dr. Seligman discovered that pessimists can change their explanatory style. By changing how we respond to failure, we can reduce the frequency and severity of depression in our life. We can also learn to get up and keep trying when we fail. Everyone faces failure! The people who do not let failure destroy their efforts to reach their dreams are far more successful.

As Seligman described these discoveries to Leslie, it became apparent to Leslie that Seligman's work was focused on helping people eliminate suffering. Seligman was focusing his energy on eliminating negatives. This was no surprise; this was the focus of the entire field of psychology and psychiatry at the time. Virtually everyone in these two fields focused on eliminating suffering – much like Tom Gardner's quote.

At this point during the plane ride, Leslie asked Seligman two very provoking questions. "Have you done much work about the other side of the coin?" "Can you predict who will never give up and who won't become depressed no matter what you do to them?" His brief answer told the whole story. "I haven't thought about them enough," he confessed.

Leslie suggested that Seligman shift his attention from pessimism to optimism, from failure to success. That is just what Seligman did. He shifted the focus of his work to the creation of positives. He shifted his work to helping people learn how to become optimists.

Research shows that optimists have an explanatory style that is just the opposite of pessimists. Optimists view success as permanent, pervasive, and personal. As a whole, they view failure as temporary, localized, and impersonal. Because of this perspective, optimists do not quit as often as pessimists. They also experience depression less often and the episodes are less severe. These differences mean everything. Studies show that optimists outperform pessimists, in addition to being healthier and happier. Optimists do better at school, sports, work, and politics. They seem to do better at everything.

Thankfully, Seligman learned that you can change your explanatory style. You can learn to become an optimist. As you become more optimistic, your tendency to quit when you experience failure will go down. As a consequence, you will experience greater levels of success.

Dr. Seligman also developed a test that you can use to identify your level of optimism or pessimism. You can use the test to find out how optimistic you are today. You can then change your explanatory style and become more optimistic. You can take the test later and see that your level of optimism improved.

*　　*　　*

After I studied Dr. Seligman's discoveries, I wondered: Is Elliot an optimist? Is that his secret? I knew that it was, but I had to prove it. To prove it, I asked Elliot to take the test.

To make sure the results of the test were accurate, I did not tell Elliot that the test measured optimism. I simply told him that the test measured the degree to which someone will be successful. Elliot agreed to take the test.

I had to wait two days before Elliot had time to take the test. On the day he was going to send me the results, I remember checking my email every hour. I was excited to find out if this was his secret – a secret he did not even know. Finally, his email arrived. I was disappointed. First, he forgot to attach the document that contained his answers to the test questions. Second, his comments in the email were not encouraging. He stated "I am not sure what this test measures, but I do not believe it measures success." He also stated "I do not believe the test is going to give you the results you were expecting."

I called him and asked him to resend the email with his test answers so that I could calculate his score. He did. My suspicions were right. Not only did his answers show that Elliot was an extreme optimist. His score was off the chart on the most important measure of optimism. The most important score on the test is called the Hope Score, which measures the degree to which you have hope. The score ranges from 0 to 16, with 0 as a perfect score and 16 as the worst. Elliot's hope score was 0. Elliot has perfect hope!

I called Elliot the next day to talk about the test results and what they meant. I explained to him that the test measured a person's explanatory style and that a person's style affected how a person responded to failure. I was completely shocked by his response. The conversation went something like this:

"Well, the test won't work for me then," Elliot said.

"Why?"

"Because I do not fail."

"You've got to be kidding," I responded. "Most people have 5 or 6 failures every week." I thought about some of my failures from the previous week. Most of us fail several times a week. We bomb an important presentation at work. We lose an important document. Someone says no when we ask them out on a date. We do poorly on a test. We have a flat tire on the way to an important event, etc., etc., etc.

"Surely you have experienced some major failures in your life," I continued.

"Show me one," he said.

"I can't think of one right now, but let's talk in a couple of days."

I was flabbergasted by the call. Not only did Elliot not see failures as personal, persistent, or permanent, he did not see them at all!

The next day I remembered a major failure in Elliot's life. When I thought about the failure, I was even more confounded by our phone call and his response. Two weeks before our phone call, Elliot had sold the largest investment that he had ever made at a loss. Elliot lost $350,000 when he sold the investment. That $350,000 represented over half of his life savings. I could not believe it. Two weeks before Elliot made the statement "I do not fail," he had lost $350,000 from a poor investment. Virtually everyone I know would have considered that a failure. Not Elliot. He simply did not use the word failure in his thinking. I was no longer confused by his long history of success.

Imagine what would happen if you could learn to think like Elliot? Imagine how many more things you would have tried. Maybe you would have tried to join that sports team at 12. Maybe you would have tried to join that local theater company at 21. Maybe you would have tried to get that job that paid far more than you make today. Imagine how you would respond if you did not even use the word failure in your thinking? How many more times would you have tried to get the goal of your dreams?

In my own life, I am sure I would have gotten another investment job after I turned down the offer from Richard Strong. If I had gotten another investment job, I would have never even been thinking about SAP. I would have made a fortune as the stock markets went straight up at the end of the 1990s.

The good news. You can learn to think like Elliot. I have and it has dramatically changed my level of success. I will discuss how later in the chapter.

*   *   *

What about Dr. Seligman? He changed the focus of his work. He changed from focusing on eliminating negatives (depression) to creating positives (optimism). How did that change of direction impact his life? Today, he is the director of the Positive Psychology Center at the University of Pennsylvania and many view him as the founder of the science of Positive Psychology. His impact on the field of psychology is reflected by the fact that he was elected President of the American Psychological Association by the widest margin in its history. He is also the author or coauthor of numerous highly successful books, including "Authentic Happiness," "The Optimistic Child," and the national bestseller, "Learned Optimism." Changing his focus towards creating positives completely changed his life.

To a large extent, Dr. Seligman has proven that we get what we believe in. If we believe life is bad, we make it bad, and it is bad. If we learn to think like an optimist, we will learn to believe that life is good, we will make it good, and it will be good.

*   *   *

How is optimism related to my transformation?

As a teenage criminal, I lived in a dark world. The darkness consumed me, tainting my view about everything. I did not want to get an education, did not want to have children, and did not want to get married. When people asked me about children, I would respond "It's a horrible world. Who would bring another child into this hell?"

My gloomy perspective wreaked havoc on the relationships that could have benefited me most. I left my childhood home at 13 and never returned, despite many attempts by my mother to bring me home. Many people tried to help me, to show me a brighter way, but I could not see it. I rewarded most of those people with trauma. Darkness surrounded my life. The face of death was my shadow. To dull the pain, I turned to drugs. I used drugs often and in large quantities. I tried to block my mind from the bleakness around me.

Today, I not only have a university education, I have a Masters degree in business. I also have a very successful career and have had the opportunity to work for several of the most respected companies in the world. Frankly, I am paid a lot of money for the work that I do. Between my work and my education, I have had the opportunity to travel to almost 200 cities in over 20 countries on 4 continents. What an amazing experience I have had! What a contrast to my dark and pessimistic teenage years.

More important than my educational and occupational achievements, I am very happily married and have five happy and healthy children. I am still somewhat surprised that my beautiful and innocent wife married me. When we were dating, I remember the night when I told her about my past. I told her that I had been arrested 14 times and had dropped out of high-school in the 10th grade. I was surprised that I got another date. When I got the courage to ask her to marry me, I remember being surprised when she said yes. She had lived a virtuous life, was getting her university education at the time, and is gorgeous. If I had focused on my failures, I would not have had the courage to ask for her hand in marriage. But she said yes, and the rest is blissful history.

My proudest achievement is the fact that child abuse does not exist in my home. I have broken the chain of child abuse that existed on both sides of my family tree for several generations. That chain of horror ended with me. I stopped it! I changed it! I learned to see a brighter world!

Today, I also have an amazing relationship with my loving mother. I try to talk to her several times a week. I listen to her and try to apply her advice. Our wounds are healed and our relationship has bloomed. Great joy has replaced sorrow. Happiness and laughter has replaced darkness and tears. If my father was still alive, I am sure I would have a great relationship with him as well. I would use all of the positive principles that I have learned to make it great.

What changed? According to the news, which usually focuses on bad events, the world appears to be in worse shape than it was when I was a juvenile criminal. Maybe the world is in worse shape, but I am not. I have achieved most of my dreams and I am making new ones. What changed? My perspective changed.

Today I firmly believe in the following quote from Sarah Ban Breathnach:

> *"Both abundance and lack exist*
> *simultaneously in our lives,*
> *as parallel realities.*
> *It is always our conscious choice which*
> *secret garden we will tend...*
> *when we choose not to focus on what is*
> *missing from our lives*
> *but are grateful for the abundance that's*
> *present /*
> *love, health, family, friends, work,*
> *the joys of nature and personal pursuits*
> *that bring us pleasure /*
> *the wasteland of illusion falls away*
> *and we experience Heaven on earth."*

In addition to looking for the good in life, I have learned two critical skills. First, I focus my energy on creating positives, not eliminating negatives. Second, I have learned to be an optimist.

*   *   *

By learning these skills I have changed my life and reached a level of success that I could not have imagined during my negative and pessimistic teenage years. Lincoln was also not born with the compassion that made him a powerful leader. In fact, when he was young, Lincoln enjoyed making fun of his enemies in public. In his early twenties, when Lincoln lived in Pigeon Creek Valley in Indiana, he would actually write letters and poems criticizing people and would leave them on public roads so that others would find them. These letters created some life-time enemies. Lincoln had clearly not yet learned how to focus his energy on creating positives.

After Lincoln started practicing law in Springfield Illinois, he would publish letters in the newspaper attacking his political opponents; a practice that was as common then as it is today. What made him stop? How did Lincoln learn to shift his energy from activities that generated hatred to ones that turned enemies into friends? Eventually, Lincoln's negative letters went too far.

In 1842, Lincoln was in a heated political battle with James Shields, the Illinois State Auditor. Like most people, Shields had made some poor decisions during his time in public office. Lincoln joined others in an effort to destroy Shields reputation and weaken his political power. Lincoln, using fake identities, published several letters in the local paper attacking Shields. Abraham Lincoln was a creative and powerful writer. In this case, he used his creative power to destroy the reputation of James Shields.

A couple of Lincoln's friends, Mary Todd and Julia Jayne, also began sending letters of their own, also using fake identities. These two got a little carried away and started to attack the character and personality of Shields by stating that he was "pompous, a hypocrite, and a liar." Others jumped into the fray and started writing letters of their own. Some of these letters recalled fictitious events at parties and social clubs that painted a poor picture of Shields.

What did Shields do? Not surprisingly, he fought back. He pressured the local paper to disclose the real names of the people who had written the letters. To protect the identity of his friends, Lincoln instructed the paper to only give Shields his name. Six years before, in 1836, Lincoln and Shields had worked together to help the state of Illinois recover from a serious financial crises. Back in 1836, Shield's believed that Lincoln was a friend. When Shields found out that Lincoln was behind the negative letter he was hurt and angry. Who wouldn't be?

Shields was determined to restore his good name. He believed that he had to take action that was both dramatic and highly visible. His reputation had been destroyed.

Drama was required to heal his public wounds. What did he do? He challenged Abraham Lincoln to a duel to the death. Partially because duels were illegal at this time in Illinois, Lincoln was shocked by the challenge and tried to avoid it. Shields would not back down. His reputation was now dead. He wanted to see something else die.

At the young age of 33, in the early morning of September 22, 1842, Abraham Lincoln crossed the Mississippi Rives at Alton, Illinois to reach a small island where he would engage in mortal combat. Some historians think they met at Blood Island, because the island was claimed by Missouri, where dueling was still legal. At 32 years old, James Shields met Lincoln on the island with a determination to restore his name or die.

Fortunately, for Lincoln, Shields, and the country, the friends who accompanied James Shields to the island talked him out of the duel. Imagine the impact on American history if Lincoln was killed or jailed for murder, instead of becoming the 16th President of the United States?

The near-duel experience had a very powerful impact on Lincoln. After that experience he rarely criticized people openly. Maintaining this gracious approach was sometimes very hard, particularly during the

Civil War. On many occasions, army leaders made big mistakes that postponed the war and increased the number of people who were killed.

Put yourself in his shoes. Imagine being the Commander in Chief of the bloodiest war in the history of your country. Imagine that you had made a personal commitment to not criticize people openly. What would you do to relieve your frustration?

This is what Lincoln did. He wrote what he called "hot letters." When he was highly frustrated or angry at someone, he would write a letter to relieve his anger. But he did not mail those letters. Instead, often he would mail a second letter expressing his appreciation and support to the person that had made the mistake. Historians have discovered several "hot letters" that Lincoln never mailed.

Abraham Lincoln is a compelling example of someone who learned to focus his energy on creating positives. We can all learn from his example.

* * *

Every day we stand before the altar of life. Every day we make promises to ourselves based on the way we act and the way we choose to look at the world. Based on your actions and attitude, what promises are you making at the altar of life? Are you spending your energy creating positive; creating good? Or, are you investing your energy trying to eliminate negatives, destroying bad? If you are committing yourself to the destruction of negatives, you are living in a tragedy.

If you are not primarily focused on creating good, how can you change your approach? Simply change your focus. For example, if you are overweight, do not focus your energy on losing weight. Pick another, positive goal that will inspire you. Run a marathon. Make a commitment to hike every major hiking path in your state. Find another positive focus that will lead to better health as a consequence. Try to join others in the pursuit of a common, positive goal. You will find even greater strength as you join others in the pursuit of good objectives.

I continue to teach in youth prisons on a volunteer basis. I teach personal transformation classes, based on the principles in this book. I am energized and inspired by the changes that I see in these youth. This effort brings me profound joy and empowers my professional work, my writing, my life. I am committed to destroying criminals by helping them transform their lives.

Obviously, there are times when you have to focus on eliminating a negative. If your kitchen is on fire, do not focus your energy on designing the kitchen of your dreams. Put the fire out first. Then design the kitchen of your dreams. Emergencies can require that we focus on eliminating negatives. The rest of the time, find ways to focus your energy on positives.

If you are pessimist, there is a cure. Dr. Seligman can help you. Read his book "Learned Optimism." Use the tools described in his book. Become an optimist and transform your life.

Whenever you embark on a journey of personal or organizational transformation remember these last two principles:

Learn to focus your energy on creating positives and learn to be an optimist.

ACKNOWLEDGEMENTS

I should have died many years ago. Most of my friends from my early teens are gone. My life was preserved and extended through a personal transformation. That transformation, and this book, was only possible through the help of many people. It is impossible for me to recognize all of them, but I cannot, in good conscience, let this book go to press without recognizing the most influential. I apologize to you, the reader, for the length of this section of the book. Frankly, this part of the book is not for you. I have to take this opportunity to thank some of the people that have helped me most and, in some cases, apologize to them.

My mother is at the top of that list. More than anyone, she tried to hold my hand when I was determined to walk on very dark and dangerous roads. Sometimes her responses were not completely rational, like the many times she picked me up at juvenile detention centers or police stations – many more times than I would have gone to retrieve a rebellious child. At other times, her actions were utterly astounding. Like the times her letters would reach me, hundreds of miles away, in some hovel or another. On several of those occasions, I remember wondering how she got my address. She often included a return envelope with her address already on it and a fresh stamp in the upper right hand corner. Sometimes she would include a return letter with check boxes and sentences next to them that said things like "Are you ok?," "Will you call me?," "What is your phone number?," "Can I send you a Christmas present?," "What size pants do you wear?" All I had to do was check a box, or enter a phone number and return the letter. I am ashamed to say that I do not remember returning any of the letters. I was in a dark hole. Thank you, Mom, for your relentless love and your forgiveness.

Next on the list are my two sisters who, because they were more than 10 years older than I, took me into their homes during some of my most tumultuous times. In both cases, I responded to their compassion with disrespect. I stole from them and brought trauma into their homes. Despite my behavior at that time, their compassion touched me. I am sorry for the pain that I caused and I thank both of you.

I am also deeply grateful for John. John came into my life through the Big Brothers Big Sisters foundation. Unfortunately, I do not remember his last name. What I do remember is this. During my blackest year, when I was 13 years old, my twisted mind convinced me that my family only helped because they had to, out of guilt. I was not convinced that they loved me. I could not use this twisted argument to explain why John was in my life. He had no reason to be motivated out of guilt. His involvement convinced me that human compassion was real. Thank you, John. You might be surprised that one of the few things I have kept through all my moves was the Erector set you gave me – the same one that your father gave you. John, if you read this please contact me. I would like to thank you in person. I also thank the Big Brothers Big Sisters foundation.

Mr. Foster was the student advisor at Morey Junior High when I was 13. He made several attempts to reach out to me right when I started my free fall into chaos. Mr. Foster went beyond the call of duty several times. I am sure that I was just one of the many troubled kids that you tried to reach. You probably do not even remember your efforts. I thank you Mr. Foster and want you to know that your efforts were not in vain. I have made attempts to contact you, but have failed. If you read this, please contact me. I would like to thank you in person.

John and Lilian Sims invited me into their home for several months when I was 16. Lilian made me breakfast, made my bed, and washed my clothes. When I was 8, my parents divorced and my mother had to juggle the role of home keeper, bread winner, and college student. No one had regularly made me breakfast, made my bed, or washed my clothes for many years. Lilian, your compassion forever touched me and helped me heal. Thank you!

Micky, I cannot forget you. It was your faith that reached over 2,000 miles and broke through the dark cloud that surrounded my mind. Because of your faith, I started to see light and that light freed me! Thank you, thank you, thank you!

Now, for the acknowledgements directly related to the contents of this book. Many of the ideas in this book are not mine. I have done my best to recognize the many people and sources that have inspired me in the Chapter Notes at the end of the book.

Writing any book is a labor of love that requires revision after revision after revision. I tortured many people with my early drafts that were so poorly written. I am grateful for the many friends that had patience as my writing matured. In particular, I want to thank Jean Draney, Ken Draper, Anne Gillis, Pam Morgan, Steve Barton, and Ron Cazier.

I also want to thank Ron Scott. Your suggestion for the book title was far more creative than my original title.

Last, but far from least, I want to thank my wife, Suzy. Thank you for your patience and support as I continue to heal from the trauma of my youth. Thank you for giving me the many nights and weekends required to write this book. Thank you for your final edits, which were some of the best. Thank you for your love.

CHAPTER NOTES

Chapter One
The Imposter

My mother kept a detailed log of several of my arrests and several of my other criminal activities described in chapter one. While I vividly remember the events, I could not have recalled all of the dates without that log. Her log is not a journal. I suspect that some of the events were too painful for her to do much more than capture the dates and minimal facts.

Some of the names in Chapter One were changed to protect the identity of people and companies that did not provide permission for their real names to be used. The school names have not been changed.

Chapter Two
Burning Boats

Wikipedia was the primary source for the details about Hernán Cortés' conquest of the Aztecs, but I also used the following books to confirm some details:

- Thomas, Hugh (1995). *Conquest: Cortés, Montezuma, and the Fall of Old Mexico*: Simon & Schuster
- White, Jon Manchip. (1971) *Cortés and the Downfall of the Aztec Empire*: Carroll & Graf

While my inspiration for using the concept of burning boats came through discussions with friends, author and motivational speaker John Boe also inspired my thinking and writing on this topic. Specifically, the quote about how the Greek's burned their boats to inspire commitment came directly from Mr. Boe's website as did the references regarding George Patton, Walt Disney, and Vince Lombardi. See http://www.johnboe.com/articles/burn_your_boat.html for more details.

None of the names in Chapter Two were changed.

Chapter Three
Trapped by a Curtain of Ideas

Wikipedia was the primary source for the details about Prague, Dresden, and Berlin, but I also used the following books to confirm some details:

- Olivová, Věra. (2000). *Dějiny první republiky, Karolinum Praha* (a Czech friend helped me with this reference)
- Taylor, Frederick. (2005). *Dresden: Tuesday, 13 February 1945*: Harper Perennial
- Maria, Ritter. (2004). *Return to Dresden*: University Press of Mississippi
- Taylor, Frederick (2006). *The Berlin Wall: 13 August 1961 - 9 November 1989*: Bloomsbury Publishing PLC

- Edwards, Lee. (1999). *The Collapse of Communism*: Hoover Institution Press

I also used Wikipedia as the primary source for details about Martin Luther, but confirmed several of the details using the following books:

- McKim, Donald K. (2003). *The Cambridge Companion to Martin Luther*: Cambridge University Press
- MacCulloch, Diarmaid (2003). *Reformation: Europe's House Divided*, 1490–1700, London: Allen Lane

The quote from Victor Hugo comes from Histoire d'un Crime (The History of a Crime) [written 1852, published 1877], Conclusion, ch. X. Trans. T.H. Joyce and Arthur Locker

While this quote from Frank Lloyd Wright is widely referenced on the internet, "An idea is salvation by imagination," I was unable to find the original source.

None of the names in Chapter Three were changed.

Chapter Four
Mind to Muscle to Metamorphosis

Most of the details on Sir Charles Sherrington came from Wikipedia. I confirmed several of the details using the following books:

- Rose, Clifford F. (2002). *Twentieth Century Neurology: The British Contribution*: World Scientific Publishing Company
- Eccles, J. (1979). *Sherrington: His Life and Thought*. Berlin: Springer International

The statistics on the use of placebos among Danish doctor's came from this source: Hróbjartsson A, Norup M. (2003) *The use of placebo interventions in medical practice--a national questionnaire survey of Danish clinicians*. Eval Health Prof. Jun; 26(2):153-65.

The statistics on the use of placebos among Israel doctor's came from this source: Nitzan U, Lichtenberg P. (2004). *Questionnaire survey on use of placebo*: British Medical Journal. Oct 23; 329(7472): 944-6.

The statements regarding the effectiveness of placebos on demonstrable diseases like herpes and ulcers came from this source: Benson, H., & Friedman, R. (1996). Harnessing the power of the placebo effect and renaming it "remembered wellness": Annual Review in Medicine, 47, 193-199.

The discussion of the link between belief and the effect of placebos on pain was presented on ABC news by Susan Donaldson James on August 1, 2007, who reported on a joint study conducted by the University of Michigan and Columbia University.

The discussion on how patients with depression showed changes in the same healing cerebral blood flow as the patients who took real anti-depressant medication came from this study: Hunter AM, Leuchter

AF, Morgan ML, Cook IA. Changes in brain function (quantitative EEG cordance) during placebo lead-in and treatment outcomes in clinical trials for major depression.

The details on how Tibetan monks generated enough body heat to dry the set sheets in near freezing temperatures can be found in the Wikipedia Tummo article.

While this quote from Lee Iacocca is widely referenced on the internet, "The greatest discovery of my generation is that human beings can alter their lives by altering their attitudes of mind," I was unable to find the original source:

The details on Benjamin Franklin and his adoption of the 13 virtues were drawn from his autobiography. The dates and details of his achievements were identified on this website: http://encyclopedia2.thefreedictionary.com/Franklin, +Benjamin

None of the names in Chapter Four were changed.

Chapter Five
The Fire Precedes the Bloom

The details on Rat Park and the Stanley Milgram experiments were primarily drawn from Chapter 2 and Chapter 7 of the following book:

- Slater, Lauren. (2005). *Opening Skinner's Box: Great Psychological Experiments of the Twentieth Century*: W.W. Norton & Co.

Several psychology studies have concluded that proximity is a major factor in determining who we become friends with in new environments, including the following:

- NEWCOMB, T. M. (1961). *The acquaintance process*: Holt, Rinehart & Winston
- Festinger, L. Schachter, S. and Back, K. W. (1950). *Social Pressures in Informal Groups: A Study of Human Factors in Housing: Harper*

As noted in the chapter, Solomon Asch conducted the conformity study in which 76% of the subjects would agree with a clearly incorrect group opinion if the group unanimously selected the wrong answer. For more details on this study see:

- Asch, S. 1958. *Effects of group pressure on the modification and distortion*. In E. E. Maccoby, T. M. Newcomb, & E. L. Hartley (Eds.), Readings in Social Psychology. New York: Holt, Rinehart, & Winston.

Several studies have been conducted which demonstrate the effects of color on our thinking, including our estimates of elapsed time, estimates of item weights, and eating behaviors. The following sources describe these studies:

- Zettl, Herbert. (1973) *Sight, Sound, Motion: Applied Media Aesthetics*. Wadworth

- Birren, F. (1952). *Your Color and Yourself*: Prang Company Publishers.
- Eysenck, H. J. (1941). *A critical and experimental study of color preferences*. American Journal of Psychology, 54, 385-394.
- Radeloff, D. J. (1990). *Role of color in perception of attractiveness*. Perceptual and Motor Skills, 71, 151-160.

The names of some of the people and companies located in Palm Desert that are mentioned in Chapter Five have been changed to protect their identity. I did not change the names for Friendly Motors or American Limousine. The company that operates under the name of American Limousine in Palm Desert today is a different company managed by a different owner. All of the other names of people and companies in Chapter Five have not been changed.

Chapter Six
Reality Slicing

The number of measurable stars in the universe was calculated by the Australian National University in the summer of 2003 (using the most powerful telescopes available at that time). The University only counted the number of stars that could actually be seen through telescopes, which means there are many more. In addition, based on the number of visible stars, there are more visible stars in the sky than grains of sand on every beach and in every desert in the world.

I could not find a conclusive source for the number of insects in the world. Based on my research, there is not even agreement on how many species of insects have been described. The few entomologists that I identified who have attempted to conduct a detailed count of even one species have found the task to be nearly impossible with current technology. For example, Paul Herbert spent several years trying to identify the unique species of moths and butterflies in New Guinea. After collecting 50,000 samples, he identified 4,100 unique species. He then tried to match the New Guinea species with the moths and butterflies cataloged at the Natural History Museum in London (the museum contains the largest collection of insects on earth, with 28 million specimens and nearly 500,000 species). After several years, he admitted defeat. He failed to identify two-thirds of his specimens. "It was like forgetting how to read," Hebert says. "It was like being struck dumb."

I used two sources to identify the number of atoms in a teaspoon of water. One was a presentation published by the Monroe County Community School Corporation in Bloomington, Indiana. The other was an online physics course published by Pearson Education.

I used the following source to confirm the quote from Isaac Newton:

- Brewster, David. (2001). *Memoirs of the Life, Writings, and Discoveries of Sir Isaac Newton*: Adamant Media Corporation

While this quote from Albert Einstein is widely referenced on the internet, "We still do not know one thousandth of one percent of what nature has revealed to us," I was unable to find the original source.

One of the names in Chapter Six was changed to protect the identity of a person who did not provide permission for their real name to be used.

Chapter Seven
Tragedy at the Altar

I used multiple internet sources to outline the relationship between Abraham Lincoln and Edwin M. Stanton, including Wikipedia. I used the following books to validate many of the details that I found online:

- Thomas, Benjamin P.. (1962). *Stanton, the Life and Times of Lincoln's Secretary of War*: Alfred A. Knopf
- Pratt, Fletcher. (1953) *Stanton, Lincoln's Secretary of War*: Norton
- Goodwin, Doris Kearns. (2005). *Team of Rivals: The Political Genius of Abraham Lincoln*: Simon & Schuster

The quotes from Abraham Lincoln's inaugural address were obtained from the Lillian Goldman Law Library of the Yale Law School.

The quotes from Abraham Lincoln's last cabinet meeting were obtained from presidentlincolnlibrary.com.

While this quote from Mother Teresa is widely referenced on the internet, "If you have a peace rally, please invite me," I was unable to find the original source:

While this quote from Albert Einstein is widely referenced on the internet, "You cannot simultaneously prevent and prepare for war," I was unable to find the original source.

All of the details on learned optimism come from Martin P. Seligman's book "Learned Optimism." Additional details on Martin P. Seligman's life and contributions came from the "Martin Seligman" and "Positive Psychology" Wikipedia articles.

The quote from Sarah Ban Breathnach is widely referenced on the internet.

The account of Abraham Lincoln leaving critical letters on the roads of Pigeon Valley is outlined in Dale Carnegies long-selling book How to Win Friends and Influence People.

The account of the confrontation between Abraham Lincoln and James Shields was derived from details outlined on the following websites, which referenced the following books:

- Wikipedia article – James Shields
- www.failedsuccess.com – The Duel that Could Have Changed the Nation
- awesometalks.wordpress.com – A Little Touch of History

- Baker, Jean H. (1987). *Mary Todd Lincoln*: A Biography: Norton
- *Webb, James R. (1975). Pistols for two...Coffee for One: American Heritage. Ed.*

There are several websites that describe Lincoln's "Hot Letters," including the following:

- http://www.huffingtonpost.com/david-quigg/how-abraham-lincolns-hot_b_225216.html
- http://mentaltesserae.blogspot.com/2008/09/hot-letters.html
- http://www.rssmicro.com/search/Abraham-Lincoln-Letters
- http://www.globalleadershipnetwork.com/Articles/Buenos_Aires.htm

Some of the names in Chapter Seven have been changed to protect the identity of people who did not provide permission for their real name to be used.

Additional books can be ordered at
www.KipKreiling.com

Please send correspondence, or requests for speaking
engagements to:

Kip@KipKreiling.com

ABOUT THE AUTHOR

A product of our broken urban society, Kip Kreiling was arrested 3 times before he was 10 and 11 times before he was 14. When Kip was only 13, he was taken out of 2 schools, a shopping mall, and a bank in handcuffs. Because of his criminal activity, and the resulting chaos in his life, Kip moved 34 times from the young age of 11 to the age of 26. On average, he moved every 5 months for 15 years, in and out of jails, group homes, and street shelters, while his mother and father moved less than 4 times each.

Today, Kip is a highly successful executive who has worked for several of the world's most respected companies, including Ford Motor, Hewlett Packard, Vodafone, and the UnitedHealth Group. As of 2009, Kip has provided transformation and business leadership services for over 40 companies in more than 20 industries. Between his corporate, consulting, educational, and speaking engagements, Kip has traveled to nearly 200 cities in 21 countries on 4 continents. Kip earned his Bachelor of Science degree at Brigham Young University and his MBA at Indiana University.

Kip Kreiling is also the founder of the non-profit foundation TransformationHelp.org. The foundation is focused on improving the human condition through personal and organizational transformation, with a focus on teaching transformation classes in prisons.

Most important to him, Kip has been happily married for almost 20 years and has five happy and healthy children. Kip Kreiling and his family live in Draper, Utah.